SMOKING
MEAT

SMOKING
MEAT

The Essential Guide to Real Barbecue

JEFF PHILLIPS

whitecap

Whitecap Books is known for its expertise in the cookbook
market, and has produced some of the most innovative
and familiar titles found in kitchens across North
America. Visit our website at www.whitecap.ca.

Publisher: Michael Burch
Editing: Taryn Boyd, Lana Okerlund and Theresa Best
Design: Setareh Ashrafologhalai and Michelle Furbacher
Photography: Michelle Furbacher
Food styling: Michelle Furbacher, Laurie Abigail Phillips,
 and Jeff Phillips
Illustrations: Setareh Ashrafologhalai

Printed in China

Library and Archives Canada Cataloguing in Publication

Phillips, Jeff, 1970-
   Smoking meat : the essential guide to real barbecue /
Jeff Phillips.

Includes index.
ISBN 978-1-77050-038-9

   1. Cooking (Smoked foods). 2. Cooking (Meat).
3. Smoked meat. 4. Barbecuing. I. Title.

TX835.P55 2012   641.6'16
C2012-901016-X

The publisher acknowledges the financial support of the
Government of Canada through the Canada Book Fund
(CBF) and the Province of British Columbia through the
Book Publishing Tax Credit.

14 15 16 17 8 7 6 5

CONTENTS

INTRODUCTION

I WAS BORN in Concord, North Carolina, but was raised all across the United States due to my dad's love for traveling, and I've always had a keen interest in food and cooking. Right out of high school and throughout college, it was not uncommon for me to treat my friends and family to food that I cooked or grilled on my little hibachi.

Just a few years after I was married, I was given a small Brinkmann smoker—the one that looks like R2-D2—and I set out to learn how to use it. I was determined to make the most of that smoker no matter how many folks told me it was cheap and hard to use. This sparked in me a love for the taste of smoked meats and a passion for barbecue tools and techniques. In this book, I share the assorted and tasty smoking adventures that followed.

I read every barbecuing book in our local library and everything else I could find on the subject, and I found myself turning out some of the best-tasting meat I had ever made. I cooked for anyone who would let me, and I would find any excuse for a get-together so I could experiment with a new type of meat to share with unsuspecting test subjects. Before long, I was being asked to cook for anniversaries, parties, and church events, and I especially loved cooking for all of my relatives on holidays.

Several years and many trial runs later, my wife, Abi, along with other members of my family, encouraged me to put all of my knowledge onto a website so I could share it with others. The more I thought about it, the more the idea made sense. From very meager beginnings, my website, www.smoking-meat.com, has grown to more than 300 pages of information on the subject, and we have 130,000 newsletter subscribers. There are 32,000 forum members

at www.smokingmeatforums.com, as well. Pretty good for something that started as a hobby.

At the beginning, I worked on the website during the evenings, and I was a manufacturing engineer at a local company during the day. But in April 2009, after being laid off from my day job due to downsizing, I decided to go into the smoking meat business full time instead of putting myself back in the job market. That was possibly one of the best decisions I have ever made.

Within the next few months I was asked to write this book and I was featured in the *Tulsa World*, our local newspaper. These events were instrumental in letting me know that smoking meat is what I was born to do. My passion became my dream job: getting paid to play with fire.

This book will equip you with the basic knowledge you need to produce succulent slow-smoked food over hot coals and wood, right in your own backyard. It is written for anyone who wants to learn more about smoking meat, regardless of whether you are a novice or a seasoned pitmaster. It will help you produce food that will make you a legend in your neighborhood and maybe even in your town.

Some of my methods may be out of the box, but others may not follow what purists have taught for years about smoking meat. I'm all about doing what works, even if it hasn't always been done that way. These pages are meant to kindle a fire in both you and your smoker, and to help you become the best pitmaster you can be.

Appréciez le voyage! (Enjoy the journey!)

When you think of smoking meat, you may be picturing old methods of curing meat whereby it is cold smoked for days or even weeks on end, which allows it to be left out of the refrigerator. That's not what this book is about. What I do is called "hot smoking": the method of simultaneously cooking and smoking meat (or other foods) at temperatures of 200°F to 250°F, in less than 24 hours in almost all cases. From this point on, when I use the short form "smoking," I am talking about hot smoking. Although I touch on cold smoking (see pages 46–47) and include a few recipes for cold smoking cheese and a few other food items on pages 207 to 210, the subjects of cold smoking and curing meats are fodder enough for books of their own.

SMOKEOLOGY

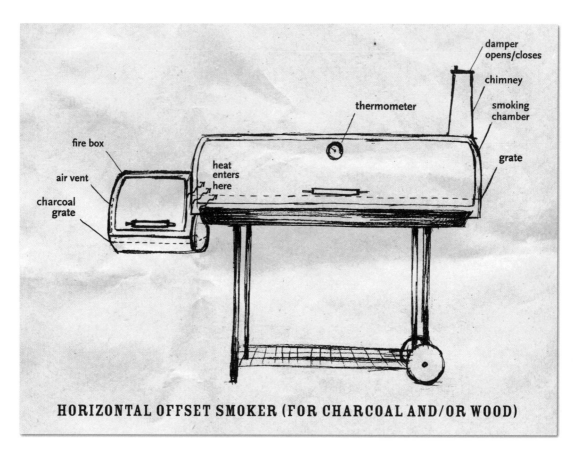

HORIZONTAL OFFSET SMOKER (FOR CHARCOAL AND/OR WOOD)

SO WHAT IS SMOKING and why is the device for it so aptly called a smoker? To make it very simple, smoking in today's world is the application of heat and real wood smoke to food to give it that comforting smoked flavor that most of us enjoy so much. There was a time when people cooked all of their food over a wood fire and the smoked flavor was the by-product of that method of cooking. Today, we have the option of cooking food in the oven, in the microwave, or on the grill, etc. with no smoke whatsoever if we so desire. To add the smoke flavor, we have to change our usual method of cooking to one that includes smoke from certain types of wood. The devices that have been designed to help make this method easier and more efficient are called smokers.

I will explain the different types of smokers and how they work, but suffice it to say that all smokers are the same in that they have a heat source fueled by wood, charcoal, gas, or electricity and, with the exception of the ones that are fueled by sticks of wood, a way to create or provide real smoke by adding chips or chunks of wood above the heat or even directly on the coals. Smokers have carefully placed vents or openings to create sufficient draft, which causes air to flow into the area of the smoker where the heat source or the firebox is located, mix with the smoke, and flow in and around the food in the smoke chamber, gently kissing it just before exiting out the other side via the chimney or exit vent. The vents are usually adjustable, to control the temperature of the smoker and/or the speed and volume of the air/smoke mixture. As you use your smoker and get used to its individual quirks, you will learn how to "make it tick" so that you can maintain the proper temperature and get the smoky flavor just the way that you and your family like it. By allowing the heat to cook the meat at very low temperatures and the smoke to flavor the meat for several hours, you will end up with some of the most tender, juicy, and flavorful meat on the planet.

Many of you may be wondering why you need a smoker when you have a grill; after all, you can get some pretty good flavor from grilling, especially when you use wood chips with the charcoal or even over the gas burners, but smoking is where tasting is believing. The secret to smoking is the long hours in which the meat has contact with the smoke. In order to use these long hours, we slow the heat down to a crawl, grab a drink, a chair, and some good music, and wait it out, knowing that the result will be worth it. I will explain how to use your grill as a smoker in later chapters, but you will have to change your thinking somewhat when it comes to outdoor cooking!

Armed with the knowledge of what smoking truly is and what a smoker is, and with the methods that I teach you in the following pages, I'm confident that you will get the best results, whether smoking meat is a fairly insignificant pastime for you or your most passionate hobby.

I'm a no-rules kind of guy when it comes to smoking meat. I'll give you some guidelines to help you get started, but I encourage you, and even expect you, to experiment wherever you feel comfortable to make these methods and recipes your own. My methods are based on my own experiences and experiments, and they don't always jive with other methods. For me, it's all

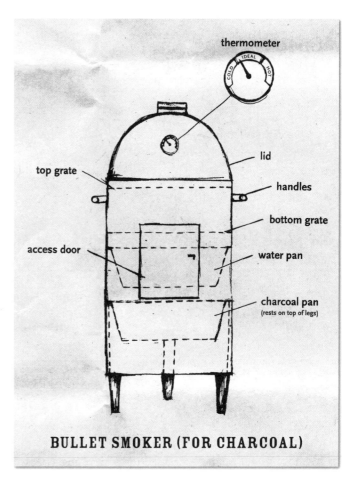

BULLET SMOKER (FOR CHARCOAL)

about flavor—whatever makes my taste buds happy. If an unconventional technique makes food taste good and it's safe, then who am I to tell you it's wrong?

TYPES OF SMOKERS

Before we get into what type of meat to cook, or consider the best fuel, or sort out the types of wood to use for flavor, I have to introduce you to the various styles of smokers so you can decide what's best for you. I have a massive collection of these things in my barn, something that makes my wife just roll her eyes. In her utter lack of understanding, she often asks, "Why do you need

Weber 22.5-inch Smokey
Mountain cooker smoker

Char-Broil Silver smoker,
barbecue, and grill

Brinkmann Cook'n Ca'jun II
charcoal smoker and grill

Lang 60-inch original
smoker

this many smokers?" I have to explain to her (all over again) that I must have these various devices so I can write reviews on them and tell other people how to make them work properly. I'm not sure she buys the story entirely, but truly, there are as many different types of smokers as there are days in a year. Fortunately, many of them share similar properties, which allows me to group them into categories.

Charcoal Smokers

The most common types of smokers are fueled by charcoal. Usually wood chips or wood chunks are added to the top of the charcoal for flavor. Although there are various styles, I've chosen to discuss the two most popular upright bullet models, as well as the do-it-yourself bullet and the horizontal offset design.

Brinkmann bullet charcoal smoker

The most basic and perhaps the most well-known charcoal smoker is the Brinkmann bullet smoker. Affectionately called the ECB or "El Cheapo Brinkmann" by many of its owners due to its low cost, this smoker can produce some really tasty barbecue. Although the ECB is very touchy and requires a lot of attention, you'll enjoy it if you're up for a challenge.

The ECB is an 18-inch barrel with three legs,

two pans, and two grates. The bottom pan is designed to hold the charcoal, and the top pan is for water or other liquids. The steam from the water pan helps to balance the heat inside the unit. Water boils at 212°F, and as the surface of the water gets hot, it starts to steam. The steam combines with the hot air in the smoker and naturally strives to regulate the ambient temperature in the smoker to 212°F.

The two grates directly above the water pan are designed to hold the meat as it cooks. I have been known to cook enough food to feed as many as 10 people on this little smoker, so don't underestimate its ability to make enough food to feed your family and guests. To amaze you even further, I can tell you that there are teams on the competition circuits who compete using only ECB smokers, and they are known to win as easily as anyone else.

This smoker requires some modification for it to work properly, but these mods are relatively easy and can be performed with basic tools and handyman skills. The recommended modifications include the following:

- Remove the legs from the inside of the barrel and place them on the outside of the barrel using the same holes and hardware. This allows the entire body of the smoker to be lifted off the charcoal pan during cooking.

Brinkmann Gourmet charcoal smoker

Brinkmann Smoke 'n Pit charcoal smoker and grill

Traeger Texas grill

Landmann 36-inch Great Outdoors Smokey Mountain propane smoker

The charcoal pan will need to sit on bricks or pavers placed under the smoker for this to work properly.

- Drill holes in the sides of the charcoal pan to facilitate better airflow to the charcoal. I recommend using a ¼-inch bit and making about eight holes in a circular pattern on opposite sides of the pan. Note that this will not only void the warranty on the smoker, but also create untimely rust. The advantage, however, is that you will be able to use it properly for a while and get some good food from your efforts. If you try to use it straight out of the box, you will most likely decide it is better suited for target practice than for cooking.

- Place a grate, about 13 inches in diameter, on the bottom of the charcoal pan to hold the charcoal (it should sit 1 or 2 inches off the bottom to allow the ash to fall down and out of the way). If you cannot find a small grate, use a double or triple layer of chicken wire cut or folded to fit about 2 inches above the bottom of the charcoal pan.

The other trick to cooking with this smoker (in addition to making the above modifications) is to use as much lump charcoal as you can fit into the firebox in order to maintain a temperature of 225°F to 240°F. If the smoker starts getting too hot, you can easily remove some of the charcoal with tongs and a good pair of heat-resistant gloves for added safety. Place any hot c oals that you remove into a metal bucket and set them aside in a safe place. You may need to add them back to the smoker later.

Weber Smokey Mountain Cooker

A smoker very similar to the ECB is the Weber Smokey Mountain Cooker (WSM). It has the same basic setup, but it has been manufactured with a lot more thought and better design. In fact, you can leave the WSM completely unattended for hours on end as it cooks your food. This makes it perfect for those long cooking sessions (as are required for brisket and pork shoulder) where it is necessary to leave the smoker running overnight in order to have the food ready by dinnertime the next day. The WSM is also used in the competition circuits by various teams, and it is very common for them to take home the prize and leave those using big fancy rigs with disappointed looks on their faces.

The price difference between the ECB and the WSM is significant, which is why so many people start out with the Brinkmann. But as they hone their skills and find themselves doing more and more smoking, they graduate to the better, but more expensive, Weber Smokey Mountain. Most

5

Temperature gauge on a Weber charcoal smoker

Access door to bottom grate, water pan, and charcoal pan

wsm users eventually become hard-core fans of the smoker, and will use nothing else after that. This speaks well for Weber and its obvious dedication to research, design, and usability.

The wsm is ready to use right out of the box. The enclosed lower section (which looks like the bottom of an egg) is the charcoal area. The charcoal grate sits down inside the lower section and a round ring with large holes sits on top of the grate.

The best way to set up this smoker for a long cooking session is to use the Minion method as described on page 25. Completely fill the ring with dry unlit lump charcoal. Place a chimney (see page 24) half full of lit charcoal on top of the dry unlit charcoal and wait about five minutes before installing the middle section (called the smoker body).

After the allotted time, carefully fit the smoker body onto the lower section. Install the water pan and fill it with water. I recommend filling it with warm to hot water in the wintertime and cool to warm water in the warmer seasons. You

will learn what works best as you use it more and more.

Set the lower and upper food grates in place and close the lid to let the smoker come up to temperature. Make sure the bottom vents are open about halfway and the top vent is fully open.

Once the smoker is at about 200°F, adjust the bottom vents so they are open about one-quarter of the way, and let the temperature slowly creep up to 225°F. It's best to let it stay on the cooler side at first, since you can easily give it more air later on to raise the temperature if necessary.

I've noticed that the temperature gauge in the lid runs about 50°F hotter than what the actual temperature is at grate level. I recommend that you test this on your own smoker so you have a better idea of any adjustments that need to be made.

Once the smoker is holding at your goal temperature, add the meat to the grate quickly and replace the lid so you lose as little heat as possible. In my experience, removing the lid allows a sudden burst of cooler air to enter the

Winch for raising or lowering grates in the drum of a homemade charcoal smoker

Homemade charcoal drum smoker

smoker. The heat will quickly come back up and stabilize once the lid is back in place.

I like to use small pieces of wood about 10 to 12 inches long and 2 to 3 inches in diameter. I place these right on top of the charcoal to create smoke. You can also use chunks of dry wood. I've found that about six pieces of 2- × 2-inch chunks or the equivalent produce the perfect amount of smoke for this smoker. As an alternative, you can mix in small chunks and slivers of your favorite smoking wood along with the unlit charcoal. This

will ensure that you have smoke throughout.

For best results, be sure to keep the water pan full of water, and remove the lid only when absolutely necessary (like when you need to baste). Never remove the lid just to look at the meat! This smoker thrives when you leave it alone and allow it to do what it does best. Patience is key.

Homemade charcoal smokers

There are also many homemade variations of the bullet charcoal smoker setup. For example, people make charcoal smokers from metal trash cans or steel drums. I won't get into how to make these, but suffice it to say that the basic vertical design works very well. If you want to find out more about these wonderful homemade contraptions, search for "drum smoker" at www.smokingmeatforums.com for a wealth of information about how to make them and where to find suitable steel drums and other hardware. With a few tweaks of these supplies, you can make some of the tastiest smoked foods you have ever had, and you will become very popular in your neighborhood at the same time.

Horizontal offset smokers

Another very popular style of charcoal smoker is the horizontal offset smoker. The Char-Broil Silver and the Brinkmann Smoke 'n Pit are two of the most popular, but there are untold numbers of other brands and models that all basically work the same way, with slight differences in metal thickness and grate size.

The design is quite simple: a large horizontal barrel is cut in half lengthwise. The top half is the lid and the bottom half is the cooking chamber where the grate sits and the meat is cooked. A smaller barrel, called the firebox, is attached to one end of and just slightly lower than the cooking chamber. A cutout between the two barrels allows the heat to pass between them. The firebox has a lid to facilitate the adding of charcoal and wood, and adjustable vents allow much-needed air to enter and stoke the fire. The larger smoke chamber usually has a 3- to 4-inch diameter chimney protruding up about 12 to 16 inches, which allows the smoke to escape.

This design requires that adequate air enters the firebox, quickly passes through the smoker, and exits the chimney at the far end of the cooking chamber. This rapid movement of air prevents the smoke from getting stale and from forming creosote on the meat or on the interior walls of the smoker.

While this style of smoker has its faults (such as uneven heating), you can, as with the upright bullet smokers, make some simple modifications that will improve its performance. One of these modifications is to place a water pan on the grate next to where the heat enters the smoke chamber. This creates steam and helps to control the heat. Another useful modification is to extend the chimney inside the cooking chamber so it's at grate level or slightly lower.

To set up this smoker for cooking I recommend preparing a single chimney (see page 24) full of lump charcoal and pouring it directly into the firebox. Leave both the firebox lid and cooking chamber lid open for about two minutes to let the heat build, then close both lids to let the heat stabilize in the cooking chamber. If the cooking chamber fails to get hot enough after about 15 minutes, consider adding another batch of charcoal to give the smoker the boost in heat it needs to meet your goal temperature.

Once the heat is holding steady within your desired range, add the meat to the grate and quickly close the lid on the cooking chamber to limit heat loss. Add a piece of wood about 2 to 3 inches in diameter and 10 to 12 inches long to the top of the charcoal. Alternatively, you can add four to six fist-sized wood chunks to the top of the charcoal to get the smoke flowing through the smoker, which will help to flavor the food you are cooking.

LEFT Brinkmann Smoke 'n Pit charcoal smoker and grill
OPPOSITE Bradley digital four-rack smoker

Bradley digital four-rack smoker

Brinkmann Gourmet electric smoker

Masterbuilt 30-inch electric smoker

Cajun Injector electric smoker

Electric Smokers

If you want to take it really easy, or if you aren't interested in tending a fire or managing hot coals to maintain a consistent temperature inside a smoker, there is hope for you. The electric smoker is about as easy as you can get; operating many such models is as simple as plugging them in and walking away. Others have rheostat or digital controllers that allow you to manage the temperature.

Brinkmann bullet electric smoker

The most basic of electric smokers for beginning outdoor cooks is the Brinkmann bullet smoker with an electric element. Like its charcoal counterpart, it has an 18-inch barrel with a water pan and two grates for food. Instead of a charcoal pan, a heating element and lava rock are at the bottom of the barrel. Wood chunks are placed around the element to provide the smoke flavor. The heat from the element warms the water in the pan above and creates steam to help control the ambient temperature in the smoker. This smoker is nonadjustable in that you cannot control the temperature by means of a dial or controller. It is designed to maintain a temperature of about 250°F at all times.

This smoker does what it is designed to do pretty well, and I have nothing derogatory to say about it. For those all-night briskets or any other meat that requires many hours of heat and smoke, this is ideal—especially if you have a hectic schedule.

I won't go into a lot of detail on this smoker, since it's about as simple as you can get. But I will say this: keep a watchful eye on the water pan. The temperature of 250°F remains consistent only as long as the water pan is full. If you let the water pan get low, the heat will begin to rise (and really spike), which just doesn't jive with the *low and slow* we're looking for. Other than that, relax and enjoy the smoke.

Cabinet-style electric smokers

Another style of electric smoker is the cabinet-style model. Two good examples are the Masterbuilt Electric Digital Smokehouse,

ABOVE Briquette feed mechanism on a Bradley digital smoker; OPPOSITE Controller on a Bradley digital smoker

commonly called the MES, and the Cajun Injector Smoker. Both look something like a small refrigerator. The top and sides are insulated, and they have a digital controller with which you can manually set the temperature. The heating element cycles on and off to maintain that temperature. Some models also have a timer with an automatic shutoff feature, and some have a very handy chute on the outside that allows you to add wood chips without opening the door. The trick to using this type of smoker is to replenish the chips every 30 minutes or so to keep the smoke flowing. This should be done for about half of the total cooking time depending on how much smoke flavor you want. For instance, if you are smoking a whole chicken, which takes about four hours at 240°F, you would add wood chips every 30 minutes for the first two hours. After that, the chicken will finish cooking with heat only.

Another well-known cabinet-style electric model is manufactured by Bradley. This smoker uses a smoke generator to create smoke from wood biscuits that look like pucks, and delivers it to the cooking chamber. Since the Bradley has two separate heating elements—a small one to convert the wood biscuits to smoke and a larger one to

control the heat inside the cooking chamber— you can also easily use it as a cold smoker for foods like cheese and fish by turning off the larger element (see more about cold smoking on pages 46–47). Each wood biscuit smokes for 20 minutes, after which it is automatically pushed into the water pan and replaced by a new one.

This easy-to-use, hands-off smoker is especially suited for all-night smoking sessions. I can tell you from personal experience that the Bradley is not just fun to work with, it also produces some very tasty vittles. I have used it to smoke ribs, meatloaf, bacon-wrapped stuffed jalapeños, and many other popular menu items with excellent results.

Traeger electric smokers

Traeger produces an electric wood smoker that uses an auger to feed wood pellets into the firepot of the cooking chamber. The pellets are ignited via an electric element and, once ignited, they provide the heat and smoke that cook and flavor the meat. This unit is also great for long cooking times, since it can be controlled with a thermostat to maintain a certain temperature. I know many folks who set these up before going to work in the morning and let them cook supper while they are gone for the day.

Propane and Natural Gas Smokers

Propane or natural gas smokers are also very common, and the concept is quite simple. Instead of a wood or charcoal fire or an electric element, a propane or natural gas tank is attached to a regulator and a burner. Once the burner is lit, wood chunks or chips are placed in a metal box over the flame. The flames from the burner provide the heat source while the smoke from the wood provides the flavor. Although it depends on the model, a water pan usually sits directly above the wood chip box; this creates a barrier between the flame and the food and adds some much-needed moisture to the air.

Great Outdoors Smoky Mountain

One of my favorite propane smokers is Landmann's Great Outdoors Smoky Mountain (also known as the GOSM). It's superb: it is easy to maintain and can create smoked meat that tastes like it was cooked on a wood-fired smoker. Brinkmann, Cajun Injector, Masterbuilt, and Char-Broil produce similar propane models.

Before you begin a smoking session, make sure your propane tank is full; I also suggest you keep a spare full tank. There's nothing worse than getting a good start on a turkey only to realize an hour later that your fire has gone out and there's no propane left in the tank, much less a spare tank in the barn. Allow this to happen on Christmas Day and you'll be stuck finishing that smoked turkey in the house. Have fun explaining that to your house full of hungry guests who fully expect to be eating that wonderful, smoke-flavored bird just like they did last year, when your turkey was the hit of the party. Yeah, been there,

OPPOSITE Landmann's Great Outdoors Smokey Mountain propane smoker

done that (in case you can't tell!). You should be able to get approximately 30 hours of use from a normal 20-pound tank of propane.

Jeff's extended instructions for propane and natural gas smokers

When I first purchased my Big Block version of the Great Outdoors Smoky Mountain propane smoker (which has a much wider body than the standard model), I noticed that the instructions included in the box left a lot to be desired. Due to the popularity of this smoker and the tons of questions I have received about it over the years, I have written some better instructions that will increase your success in the use of this smoker. (These instructions will also work with other propane and natural gas smokers.)

1. Hook up the propane tank and make sure it is snug. The newer 20-pound tanks all have a large, black-handled knob that uses normal right-handed threads to tighten the connection to the propane tank.
2. Open the door of the smoker by turning the handle 90 degrees counterclockwise. Remove the smoker box and fill it to the top with dry wood chips or chunks. Replace the lid on the smoker box and return it to the wire-framed cradle just above the burner where you removed it originally.
3. Line the water pan (located just above the chip box) with a large piece of heavy-duty foil. Make a habit of this step to save a lot of time. Instead of cleaning all the goo that accumulates in the water pan, you can simply remove and discard the foil, leaving a clean water pan ready for your next smoke.

4. Go into the house (or, if you're lucky, to the sink in your outdoor kitchen area) and fill a ½-gallon pitcher full of hot water. Pour the water into the foil-lined water pan.

5. Now for the fun part! Turn the large knob on the left a few clicks and make sure it is emitting a spark next to the burner. If there is no spark, remove your hand from the knob and feel below the control area (the area just below the two knobs) for a wire; make sure it's securely connected, then try turning the knob again. IMPORTANT: Do not touch the wire while you are turning the knob or you may have a shocking experience! If the burner sparks properly, turn the right-hand knob to high and immediately turn the left-hand knob a few clicks to ignite the propane burner.

6. While the smoker is coming up to temperature, you need to make sure the vents are set properly. If you have the type with two lower vents, close them as far as the tab stops will allow (which is the "GOSM way" of helping you avoid the mistake of closing the vents all the way), then set the top vent to the same position (closed at the tab stop). If you have the type with only the top vent, simply set it to closed (at the tab stop). I know some folks who have learned that with certain milder woods they can get more smoke flavor by bending up the stops and closing the vents a little more. For now, leave them be and stay on the safe side. IMPORTANT: On *any* smoker, it's crucial to set the vents correctly to allow proper airflow in and out of the smoker. This allows your fire to burn properly, and lets the smoke "kiss" your meat instead of settling on it and building up creosote.

7. Let the smoker continue to burn on high for about a minute, then set the heat control knob between low and medium to allow the temperature to settle in at 225°F.

8. The wood will start smoking in about four or five minutes, or maybe even sooner, so you want to get your meat into the smoker quickly. If I'm smoking only a small amount, I use the rack that sits at the same level as the thermometer, just to make sure I know what the exact temperature is at meat level. If I'm loading it down, I leave a little room around each piece of meat to allow plenty of airflow, which ensures everything is smoked properly.

9. Once you have the meat in the smoker, close the door and latch it by turning the handle 90 degrees clockwise.

10. Sit back for about an hour or so with your favorite beverage, checking the smoker occasionally to make sure it is maintaining your target temperature or to make small adjustments to the heat control knob (higher or lower as necessary). You'll find that it sometimes takes as much as two or three minutes for the temperature to level out once you make a change, so make a very small adjustment and wait to see what happens. With practice, you'll learn exactly where to set the knob to maintain a specific temperature. You'll also notice a difference based on how much meat you are cooking; a smoker full of cold meat will need more heat to reach and maintain your target temperature than a smoker with, say, only one pork butt in it.

11. After about 90 minutes you'll probably need to add more wood chips or chunks to the chip box. (A telltale sign that it's almost time to add more wood is when the smoker starts smoking heavier than usual.) Quickly and carefully open the door and, using heavy-duty tongs (big channel-lock pliers also work great)

and a welding glove or other heat-resistant glove, pull out the chip box carriage. Remove the lid and then the chip box with the tongs or pliers, and set them on the ground. Quickly close and latch the door so the smoker maintains its temperature while you are replacing the wood chips or chunks.

12. Pour the ashes and pieces of coal still in the chip box into a metal container, making sure nothing flammable is in the vicinity.

13. Refill the chip box with chunks or chips and return it to the chip box carriage in the reverse order of removal as quickly as possible to minimize heat loss. For ribs and poultry you'll probably need to refill the chip box only a couple of times, but for larger cuts like brisket and pork butt you may need to do it three or more times. A good rule of thumb is to keep refilling the chip box until the temperature of the meat reaches 140°F.

14. When the meat is almost done based on the reading of a digital probe meat thermometer (see the Master Table of Smoking Times and Temperatures on page 48) or a tenderness test (see sidebar), get yourself another cold beverage and hang out around the smoker so you're ready to pull the meat out when it reaches its moment of perfection.

Wood-Fired Smokers

I think everyone will agree that the taste of meat cooked on an authentic wood-fired smoker is unbeatable in every way. The time spent building, tending, and poking the fire just appeals to the inner Neanderthal in all of us. And believe it or not, a certain part of our brain is put into a trance-like state when we watch flames dancing upon wood. Aside from the psychological aspect of it, the intense flavor of meat cooked over a real

TENDERNESS TEST FOR RIBS
Most smoked meats are cooked to a certain temperature at which they are safe to eat, but ribs are cooked until they are tender (which usually happens long after they are "done" in terms of temperature). To check tenderness, pull two of the rib bones in opposite directions. If the meat tears easily, the ribs are ready to eat.

wood fire is second to none.

I personally enjoy cooking on a wood-fired smoker more than on any other kind, but it is labor-intensive. You can't walk away for too long because you need to adjust a vent or add a stick of wood quite often. I usually reserve cooking on my wood smoker for days when the weather is good and I have other things I can do outdoors and close by—but it can also be a great excuse to grab your favorite beverage and a lawn chair and just treat yourself to some real rest and relaxation.

Most wood-fired smokers are built very similarly to the horizontal offset charcoal smoker, with a large cooking chamber for the meat and a slightly smaller area on the side known as the firebox. A vent lets air into the firebox and a chimney protruding up from the cooking chamber allows the air/smoke mixture to exit.

There are two types of wood-fired smokers built in this horizontal offset fashion: the direct flow and the reverse flow. In the direct flow style, the heat and smoke flow from the firebox directly into the cooking chamber through a semicircle-shaped hole. The smoke travels immediately up to the grate where it cooks and flavors the meat. Some smokers have a baffle that directs the heat and smoke downward.

In my experience, the temperature in the direct flow type of smoker is not as balanced as in the reverse flow. The latter is so named because of the way the heat and smoke flow out of the firebox, under the grate, and all the way to the far end of the cooking chamber before finally rising and moving across the grate to the open chimney on the firebox side of the smoker. This reverse flow is made possible via a heavy steel plate welded just under the grate, which forces the heat and smoke to stay down until reaching the far end

of the smoker. The metal plate tends to absorb some of the heat, and this helps to balance both the temperature inside the cooking chamber and the movement of air through the smoker. Many fans of the reverse flow style feel a balanced temperature is paramount in cooking great food, whether for home use or in competitions.

I have used both types of wood-fired smokers and, while I prefer the reverse flow design, both styles are widely used. More important, each can be fine-tuned to produce the tastiest and most mouthwatering food on the planet.

Smoking on a Grill

So, you don't have a smoker but you *do* have a grill, and you are wondering if there is possibly some way you could . . . I can read your mind, and the answer is an emphatic yes! You can absolutely use your gas or charcoal grill to smoke meat using a few simple techniques. You must fully understand that smoking meat is all about *low and slow*. But for now, just know that any form of smoking must be done with low, indirect heat.

Indirect heat on a grill is achieved by placing the meat on one side of the grill while the heat source is on the other side. On a gas grill, this can mean turning on the leftmost burner and placing the meat on the right side of the grate. You could also turn all burners on high to get the grill up to temperature, then adjust the heat by leaving only one burner on. Or, if your grill has three burners, you could turn off the middle burner and place the meat in the center of the grate.

To achieve a smoky flavor, wrap some wood chips in foil and place them above one of the burners; poke a few holes in the foil packet to allow the smoke to escape easily. Alternatively, you can purchase a smoker box to hold the wood chips from Home Depot, Lowe's, Amazon.com, or any place that sells smoking and grilling supplies.

It may take 15 to 20 minutes for the chips to start smoking properly on a gas grill, but I have a special technique for dealing with this: place the wood chip package or smoker box filled with chips directly over the burner you are using for heat. Turn the burner on high and leave the lid of the grill open until you see smoke. At this point, you can add the meat to the grill (on the opposite side to the heat source), close the lid, and turn the heat down to medium to maintain a temperature of 225°F to 240°F.

If you need more smoke, start with two wood chip packages or smoker boxes instead of one, and follow the same technique. Don't soak the wood—this just creates steam initially and prolongs the time it takes for the real smoke flavor to emerge.

In a hurry? I've been known to place the wood chip package or smoker box directly over the flame on my side burner to get it going faster.

Once I see it smoking really well, I use barbecue tongs to set the wood chip package directly over the burner I'm using for heat.

To smoke meat on a charcoal grill (like the famous Weber grill), you can place a metal drip pan in the center of the grill (under the grate) with hot charcoal placed evenly on either side. Place the meat directly above the drip pan. For longer cooking sessions, place water in the drip pan to help balance the heat inside the grill and to keep the drippings from burning. Wood chips or chunks should be placed on the charcoal for smoke flavor.

What Kind of Smoker Is Right for You?

Many other models of smokers are made by various companies, and all work similarly to the ones I have mentioned. Amazon.com is a good source of information and reviews about all types of smokers. There is also a Smokers & More section at www.smokingmeatforums.com, where you can find reviews and ratings of various smokers and equipment. The really nice thing about this resource is that the reviews and ratings are all created by forum members.

The smoker you purchase is entirely up to you, but your choice should be guided by the number of people you want to feed, whether you live in a house or an apartment, and the amount of time that you have available to cook. For instance, someone with a very busy lifestyle might want to consider a set-it-and-forget-it style of electric smoker, such as the cabinet models made by Bradley or Masterbuilt. Someone living in an apartment complex with restrictions on patio fires may also choose an electric smoker. Others may have more flexibility. My advice is to do your research and identify the factors important to you before making a purchase decision.

FUEL: CHARCOAL, GAS, OR WOOD?

Charcoal

Not all charcoal is created equal. Even similarly marked bags of the two main forms—lump charcoal and charcoal briquettes—have differences in burn time, burn quality, moisture level, and overall quality. Bigger price or bigger name doesn't necessarily equal better charcoal. It pays to read reviews and do some testing to see what works best.

I'm not a big fan of charcoal briquettes, since it is well known they are sometimes made from questionable ingredients. I'm not saying that I never use charcoal in briquette form, but it is very rare and usually because I need a very steady heat for a long period of time, such as when I'm using the Minion method (page 25) and I don't have the time to babysit the smoker.

Unfortunately, lump charcoal does not always provide the consistent burn you get from the evenly sized briquettes. Other than that, lump charcoal is the all-around best option. It is simply wood that has been burned in a low- or no-oxygen environment. Some say that lump charcoal burns hotter and faster, but I haven't seen any official evidence for this. One major advantage to using lump charcoal is that it is manufactured from pure wood and doesn't contain the fillers and other chemicals found in briquettes. Lump charcoal also produces significantly less ash, which tends to smother a fire during long burn times. If you don't use charcoal in lump form, you have to find a way to let the ash drop below the charcoal. Disadvantages of lump charcoal are that it is usually more expensive than briquettes, the pieces are inconsistent in size, and it tends to spark when poured into the charcoal pan or firebox.

Gas

Propane and natural gas are both excellent fuels for smoking meat. Both burn very cleanly and are very easy to acquire. Propane can be purchased in exchangeable tanks at gas stations, feed stores, and retailers like Walmart—or perhaps, like me, you've got a 500-gallon propane tank in the backyard to which you can hook up directly.

In most parts of the United States and

elsewhere, natural gas is piped directly to individual homes. An outside connection can easily be established by someone certified to work with natural gas lines; this will ensure you always have a ready supply of fuel available.

I don't use natural gas to fuel my smokers, so I can't comment on the gas usage of these models; however, based on my personal data, you should get about 30 hours of use from a 20-pound (5-gallon) propane cylinder.

Wood

Meat smoked with wood, and wood only, is unlike anything you have ever tasted. If you have the option of using all wood, consider yourself very lucky. Not everybody has the luxury of using only wood in their smokers, for some of the following reasons:

- Many smokers are too small and are not designed to be used with all wood.
- Wood may be unavailable, too expensive, or difficult to transport.
- Your neighborhood or complex may not permit the storage of wood and/or open fires.

These challenges aside, wood-fired smokers are well worth the time and money you'll invest.

Woods for smoking

The wood that is available to you depends on where you live. The general rule is that if a tree bears a nut or a fruit and is a hardwood, its wood can be safely used for smoking (though this doesn't guarantee that you'll like the flavor it provides, or that it will complement the meat you are smoking).

I find myself using a lot of cherry these days—on almost everything—so that could possibly be my all-time favorite wood for smoking. My preferred woods for smoking are:

- cherry
- oak
- mesquite
- pecan

On the next page is a list of some of the woods I have used for smoking, with my notes. I highly recommend that you make your own notes on each wood you try so you can remember what type of meat you used it with and whether or not you liked the flavor it imparted.

WOODS FOR SMOKING

Wood	Notes
Alder	Very light flavor, great for smoking fish
Apple	Very light flavor
Apricot	Sweet and fruity
Cherry	Good solid flavor, but not overpowering; my favorite wood for smoking
Hickory	Known to be the king of all woods for smoking; strong, pungent flavor
Maple	Sweet bacon-like flavor; excellent for pork
Mesquite	Very strong, earthy flavor; great for beef; use sparingly
Oak	Medium flavor; works great as a base wood when you just need heat
Olive	Smells and tastes like olive oil; very good for chicken and pork
Orange	Sweet and fruity; great for chicken and pork
Peach	Sweet and fruity; great for pork
Pecan	Good solid flavor; similar to hickory but not as pungent
Plum	Sweet and fruity; somewhat mild flavor; try it with turkey
Walnut	Can be strong; use with some caution

OTHER WOODS THAT ARE GOOD FOR SMOKING

- Acacia
- Almond
- Ash
- Bay
- Beech
- Birch
- Black cherry
- Butternut
- Chestnut
- Cottonwood
- Crab apple
- Fig
- Grapefruit
- Grapevine
- Guava
- Hackberry
- Lemon
- Lilac
- Mulberry
- Nectarine
- Pear
- Persimmon
- Pimento
- Willow

I'm not an authority, but conventional wisdom is that resinous woods will produce an acrid flavor and could make you ill. If you have used resinous woods and you did not get sick, then more power to you, but I don't plan on taking any chances on ruining meat or making someone ill.

WOODS NOT SUITABLE FOR SMOKING

The following woods are resinous and should *not* be used for smoking:

- Elm
- Eucalyptus
- Fir
- Liquid amber
- Pine
- Redwood
- Spruce
- Sweet gum
- Sycamore

Many people say that cedar should not be used for smoking meat, although it is used quite commonly in the form of soaked planks on which you place meat for the grill. The

Cherry   Pecan   Apricot   Oak

consensus is that a cedar plank soaked in water for many hours before use doesn't burn up, but only smokes lightly. Based on my research, the smoke composition of a burning piece of wood does seem different than of wood that is smoking lightly on the grate above the flames of a grill. I am not a scientist and I don't claim to be an expert on the matter, so I will leave this for you to decide. I have received e-mails from folks who use cedar in their smokers, and while I cannot argue with this, I will say that if you plan to do the same, proceed with some caution.

Let me also warn you against using woods used for construction, such as lumber scraps, railroad ties, and landscape timbers, as these are commonly treated with chemicals.

Finding wood

I am often asked about the best way to acquire wood. While I don't have a certain answer for every area of the country, I can tell you what works for me (and I tend to have a never-ending supply of wood that rarely comes from my 10 acres of pecan trees). The icing on the cake is that most of these suggestions have the word "free" attached to them. Just keep in mind one thing: you will need to store freshly cut (i.e., "green") wood in a dry

area, such as in a barn, in a shed, or even under a tarp, to dry or "season" for four to six months before you can use it for smoking.

FRIENDS AND NEIGHBORS. That's right. Ask your friends, neighbors, and even your coworkers if they know anyone who might have some wood they don't want or would sell for cheap. This can be a great way to let folks know you are looking, and even if you don't find what you want right away, people will most likely remember you and contact you if it becomes available.

CRAIGSLIST, NEWSPAPER CLASSIFIEDS, AND LOCAL BUY/SELL MAGAZINE. You'll find folks who sell wood, and some of them may even deliver it for a small fee. Be sure to ask what kind of wood it is, where they got it, and whether it is green or seasoned. The type of wood is especially important, since you can use only hardwood. Coniferous woods like pine and spruce aren't food-worthy and can even make you sick if you use them for smoking. If sellers act like they don't know what kind of wood they have, consider that a red flag.

In the same vein, you can place an ad on Craigslist, in your local newspaper classifieds, or

Many folks have asked me if they should remove the bark from wood before using it for smoking. The claim commonly found on the Internet is that wood bark can impart a bitter taste to meat, but I just can't validate this claim based on my personal experience. The only time I remove bark is if it is already loose and ready to come off, or if it looks moldy, appears diseased, or has something on it such as a fungus, moss, an insect, or a worm. In general, I don't worry too much about bark.

even on the bulletin board at your local grocery store. Let folks know that you'll clean up and haul away fallen trees and limbs. You can also let them know what kind of wood you're interested in if you're feeling lucky.

ORCHARDS. Orchards are great places to stop and ask for wood. You might just find yourself hauling away a truckload of the good stuff, since they seem to prune limbs constantly. If they don't have any at the time you ask, they should be able to tell you when they will.

STOP AND ASK. Drive around town or your neighborhood and look for downed trees, especially after storms. Knock on doors and boldly ask if you can have the wood. The worst thing someone can say is no, and that's no skin off your back. I was just talking to my neighbor the other day, and he mentioned that beavers were making a mess of all the pecan trees around his creek. He was planning to cut all of the saplings down and burn them. To me this was a call to action, and I immediately asked if I could relieve him of this duty. Of course he happily agreed, and I'm now the proud owner of several years' worth of pecan logs that are perfectly sized for my smoker. You know the saying: one man's junk is another man's treasure.

BUILDING AND MAINTAINING A FIRE
Wood Fire

Boy and Girl Scouts are really good at building fires on the fly, and while theirs is a surefire method of fire-building, lots of other methods work equally well. I am going to describe a few different ways to get the job done, and you can then choose what works best for you, or even develop your own unique method.

Until just a short while ago, I always used a technique that is very similar to the Boy/Girl Scout method: dry kindling on the bottom in a teepee fashion, paper under and around the kindling, then larger and larger pieces of wood until you have the size of fire you want. Nowadays, I tend to use several different methods depending on what I am doing and whether I am building a fire in my large wood burner, in one of my smaller units, or in the fireplace.

Boy/Girl Scout method

1. Start with a heaping handful of dry kindling; this can be slivers of wood, pine needles, or very small twigs. I can see it now: several of you are scratching your heads and wondering what a "heaping handful" is. Well, it's such a big handful that it's falling out of your hand.

2. Form the kindling into a teepee. If you're fortunate enough to have long, dry slivers of wood, place some dry pine needles or dry grass under and around the base of the teepee. Since we aren't out in the woods, you can also use newspaper. And if you really want to veer from the authentic method of fire-building, you can pour a little olive oil on the newspaper, which will help it to burn better and longer.

3. Light the kindling. Once it is burning really well, place some slightly larger sticks over the smaller kindling, maintaining the teepee form. Continue adding larger and larger pieces of wood until you have a fire that is able to produce the heat you need in your smoker.

Traditional method

1. Place two medium-sized (no more than 5 inches in diameter) pieces of wood parallel to each other on the bottom of the firebox, leaving about 8 inches between them.

2. Lay two slightly smaller pieces on top of and perpendicular to the first two. Build about four levels in this pattern, making sure the logs on each level are slightly smaller than the ones below them. This leaves an open area in the center that is about 8 inches square.

3. Place dry kindling, paper, and fire starters in this open central area.

4. Light the kindling. As it gets going, it will

immediately begin working on the larger stuff, so you will get a bigger fire a little faster than with the Boy/Girl Scout method.

Upside-down method

This method—in which everything seems backwards—requires you to forget everything you think you know about building a fire.

1. Place four logs, each about 5 inches in diameter, on the bottom of the firebox as close to each other as possible.

2. On top of and perpendicular to the first layer, place four or five slightly smaller split logs very close together.

3. On top of the first two layers, place as many

Propane weed burner

Charcoal Fire

Most of us have our own favorite ways of getting a charcoal fire started. When I was a child, it was always fun to watch my dad douse charcoal with an entire bottle of lighter fluid and then light a match and fling it onto the grill. He always had to jump back pretty quickly to avoid being left without eyebrows, beard, and arm hair for several weeks.

While this is a common way to start a fire—and brings out the inner pyromaniac in all of us—it is not really the best, and is certainly not the safest, way to get the charcoal burning. I hope I can persuade you to use any of the following tools, which allow for much better and safer fire-starting methods.

Charcoal chimney

A charcoal chimney is a round metal device that resembles a coffee can with a large handle. Charcoal is placed in the top and newspaper in the bottom. When the newspaper is lit, it in turn lights the charcoal. Within just a few minutes the charcoal will be white hot and ready to pour into the firebox.

While the above method is simple and works really well, I have discovered an even easier way to use this tool if you happen to have a gas grill with a side burner. Fill the charcoal chimney with charcoal and set it on the burner. Light the burner, and once the charcoal is lit simply turn the burner off. You will soon have an entire batch of charcoal ready to pour into the firebox.

Wax fire starters

Wax fire starters are blocks made of wax mixed with wood sawdust and fibers. They come in various types and sizes, and can easily be lit and placed under or slightly to the side of unlit

small sticks, each about 1½ inches in diameter, as will fit. The sticks should be perpendicular to the layer beneath.

4. Fold a section of newspaper in half and then in half again, and lay it flat on top of the wood. For a better burn, you can pour some olive oil on the paper.

5. Pile some very small kindling on top of the paper, then light the paper and wait for it all to happen. The paper starts burning and very quickly lights the kindling. Within just a few minutes the kindling is blazing and your job is done. I don't know exactly why it works, but the kindling lights the wood below it, and that wood lights the next layer, and so on. This setup will burn for hours on end, unattended—happy news for anyone who wants a fire, whether that be in the smoker or in the fireplace.

No matter which method you choose to build your fire, some practice is required to learn how much wood you should start with in order to maintain a 225°F to 240°F temperature in your smoker. Only experience can teach you that.

charcoal. These starters will generally burn for 10 to 15 minutes, which is plenty of time to light the charcoal. Make sure the ones you purchase are safe for use in a barbecue, since some varieties are designed to be used in a fireplace, and contain chemicals or additives. Read the information on the package before purchasing.

Propane weed burner

This little gizmo is simply a long neoprene hose that connects to a propane tank, with a wand at the other end. Once lit, a flame jets out from the wand that is fit for killing weeds, terminating anthills, and starting charcoal. I think men probably have way too much fun with this toy, but it does a great job at getting charcoal blazing within minutes.

Minion method for maintaining a charcoal fire

As I understand it, Jim Minion discovered this awesome method for keeping a charcoal smoker hot for hours on end during a moment of sudden inspiration. This method is sheer genius, and in the smoking world, Jim will forever be a legend.

In a nutshell, a single chimney (see previous page) of lit charcoal is poured on top of a large pile of unlit charcoal. Over time, the lit charcoal slowly lights the charcoal below it. This method, when set up correctly, can produce constant heat for as long as 16 hours. This allows for that much-needed sleep during the long cooking times required by large cuts of meat such as brisket and pork shoulder.

There are some basic technical requirements for this method to work. The unlit charcoal must have access to plenty of air from the bottom and sides. For this reason, most people who use this method build a charcoal holder from expanded metal or a similar material; legs on the

Charcoal chimney

holder let it sit at least 3 inches above the bottom of the smoker.

Remember that each smoker is different, and it may take a little practice to discover exactly how much lit charcoal is required to maintain the desired smoker temperature and how much unlit charcoal is required to maintain that heat across a certain number of hours. But with some patience, perseverance, and good note-taking, the Minion method can easily allow you to leave the smoker unattended while you sleep or take care of other things. The Weber Smokey Mountain Cooker is especially well suited (out of the box) for this method.

TOOLS AND EQUIPMENT

There are many more smoking gadgets on the

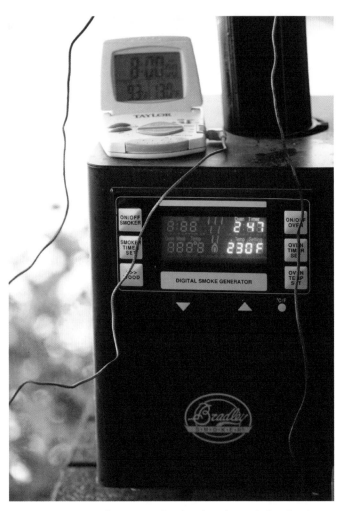

Controller on a Bradley digital smoker, with digital probe meat thermometer

temperature of meat. Instead, they've learned how to tell the temperature by how the meat looks and feels. I have nothing against this method, but it is not necessarily very accurate. I prefer the scientific approach in which technology determines the exact internal temperature of that pork loin or Thanksgiving turkey or whatever it is I happen to be cooking. Don't take this the wrong way; if you can hit the nail on the head every time you look at and feel meat, then I envy you, but since most of us cannot do that, I highly recommend the use of a good instant-read, digital probe meat thermometer.

Digital meat thermometers are inexpensive (they can cost as little as $15), and can be purchased almost anywhere cooking tools are sold. You can also pay a little more if you want something nifty—a remote version that allows you to keep the monitor with you while the probe stays in the meat, for example. This is actually a pretty sweet device, and I highly recommend obtaining one if you can afford it.

Insert the thermometer into the meat in the early stages of the cooking session, and leave it there while the meat cooks. The braided metal cord can be placed in the doorjamb of the smoker or inserted through a hole or vent. The actual probe itself should not touch metal of any kind, or it can short out and cease to work (you can purchase replacement probes). With a little care, thermometers can last for many years. I have about six of them, and all still work as well as they did the day I bought them.

The probes can also be used to test the ambient temperature of the smoker. Simply insert the probe through a potato, allowing about 2 or 3 inches of the probe to stick out the other side. Place the potato on the grate along with the meat, and you'll have an accurate reading of the heat

market than I could ever hope to mention in a single book. Below, I have selected the ones I feel are the most useful for a basic setup. As you advance in your skills, you may choose to expand your collection of smoking gadgets. Trust me when I say that this can become very addictive.

Thermometers and Temperature Control

I know many, many chefs who absolutely refuse to use a thermometer to test the internal at grate/meat level. Feel free to eat the smoked potato later.

I see many novice pitmasters using mechanical or digital instant-read thermometers that are designed to pierce the meat and check its internal temperature during the cooking session, but that cannot be left in. These are not good, and I will explain why: every time you pierce, poke, or otherwise insert an object into very hot meat, the tasty juices bubble out of the hole you just made, and that is never a good thing. You need those tasty juices to remain inside the meat. I recommend you place the digital probe meat thermometer into the meat halfway through your cooking session, and do not remove it until the meat is out of the cooker and has rested for 15 to 30 minutes. The meat will seal around the probe early on and the delectable juices will stay inside, while you still get a constant read on the internal temperature of the meat.

Food safety and thermometers

Here's a little food safety tidbit for you while we are on the subject of thermometers: I used to recommend that the thermometer be inserted into the meat when it is first placed in the smoker. However, recent studies on ways to prevent bacteria and foodborne illnesses seem to suggest that if bacteria is present on the surface of the raw meat and a thermometer or any other object is inserted, it could carry that bacteria deep into the meat and create a real safety issue.

My understanding is that the temperature must reach 140°F a half-inch below the surface of the meat within the first four hours of a cooking session in order for it to be safe to eat. I can say with certainty, based on years of experience, that a meat temperature of 140°F is easily accomplished within four hours of cooking at

225°F for all types of meats. That's why I suggest inserting the thermometer into the meat halfway through a cooking session.

You might already be wondering whether this rule also applies to injecting marinades or other liquids into the meat (see page 37) or making incisions of any kind before the interior reaches 140°F. I try not to get too carried away with this. I often inject raw meat with marinades and I sometimes insert the thermometer at the beginning of the smoking session. I mention this information only because it's one way to add an extra safety net into your cooking techniques.

Stoker Power Draft System

A while back I heard of an electronic device that operates a blower attached to your charcoal or wood-fired smoker in order to maintain a certain temperature level. I contacted the company and they promptly sent me a test model to try out on my 22½-inch Weber Smokey Mountain Cooker.

This thing is serious geek candy; it comes with all the bells and whistles you would expect. You can connect it to your home computer network and use it to monitor online both the temperature of your smoker and the internal temperature

of your meat. What's more, you can control the temperature of your smoker online! For my first test, I set up my smoker for about 225°F, then set the Stoker to maintain that temperature. I watched intently for over an hour as the fan cycled on and off, on and off, and maintained the temperature within mere degrees. I finally went to take care of other things, returning five hours later to some of the best ribs I have ever eaten. The only thing on my mind at that moment was, "I could sure get used to this!"

I am "stoked" about this piece of equipment. While there are no doubt other devices that do a similar job, this seems to be the one that everyone is talking about, and from the only company that offered to send me a test model. To find out more about the Stoker, visit Rock's Bar-B-Que's website at www.rocksbarbque.com.

Cooking Utensils

Every backyard chef needs a good set of tools. It doesn't have to be an expensive set, but it does need to be sturdy enough to stand up to a little abuse. I recently received a new set of stainless steel, heavy-duty barbecue tools as a gift, yet I still prefer the cheapo set I have been using for years and years. It's not about price, or even what material the tools are made of. The utensils must be useful, and I think that is judged from a personal perspective. What works best for me may not work best for you.

Tongs

The most useful tool I own is my tongs. I use tongs to flip meat, place meat on the grate, place a chunk of wood in a precise spot, add or remove charcoal from the firebox, move the grate when it is hot—the list goes on and on. I truly believe that I could not cook without them. Make sure your tongs completely close at the tip, or you will find yourself wishing they did at some point.

Spatula
Another wonderful tool that is a must for any outdoor cook is a heavy-duty spatula. It needs to be sturdy enough to slip under a heavy piece of meat, like brisket, and lift it without bending. I often use my spatula in tandem with my tongs to flip a brisket and/or remove it from the smoker when it is finished cooking.

Basting brush and saucepot
I would be remiss if I failed to mention the basting brush and its companion 1½-cup saucepot. The best brushes have silicone bristles, which do a great job of holding the sauce as you move it from the pot to the meat. The saucepot should be stainless steel. Both the brush and saucepot can be thrown into the dishwasher after use. You can also use a sauce mop for basting; most are bristled like a paintbrush, though others resemble miniature floor mops. Try a few out and see what works best for you.

Knives
I am not sure if knives would normally be considered cooking utensils, but I'm going to categorize them as such and recommend that you get a good set, along with a sharpener. I prefer to use certain knives when cutting ribs, others for chopping veggies, and still others for slicing brisket or deboning chicken.

When people ask me what the best knives are, I always say, "sharp ones." That really is the best answer. Different brands of knives definitely differ in quality, but a cheap knife that is sharp will work better than a high-quality one that is dull. No matter what type of knives you choose to

use, learn how to sharpen them, then keep them sharp. Many chefs sharpen their knives before each use, and while most of us aren't professional chefs, there is something to be said for having properly maintained tools.

Grill brush and scraper
A grill brush and scraper combination is an excellent utensil to have in your barbecue toolbox. All of that gunk that sticks to the grates can easily be knocked off with one of these. I usually replace mine a couple of times each year, or more often if necessary. This tool should be used to clean the grate after each smoking session. After cleaning my grate, I like to spray it lightly with oil to get it ready for the next use.

Spray bottle
Another must-have tool is a spray bottle. These bottles are great for spraying meat with various liquids as it cooks; for example, ribs with apple juice, or turkey with melted butter. The applications are endless, and you'll find yourself using the bottles over and over.

I found some small spray bottles in the beauty supplies section of my local department store. I purchased several in varying colors to help me remember which liquid is in each bottle. You can also just as easily label each bottle to show that it contains apple juice, olive oil, water, or whatever you like to use.

Gloves and Aprons

When working with burning charcoal, flaming wood, and sizzling hot meat, it's necessary to protect your hands and clothing. For this reason, folks have put their heads together to come up with wearable items that protect you and your clothing from heat and splatters that naturally occur during cooking. While you can possibly cook and smoke meat without these items, they are in the "nice to have" category. At a minimum, I highly recommend buying a good set of heat-resistant gloves (that go up to your elbows) and an apron that will keep your clothes free of grease and food splatters. I prefer an apron with lots of pockets for carrying thermometers, cooking utensils, pencils, and seasonings.

I feel that Weber has done the best job of producing well-thought-out items that fit into this category. I love their long, thick, heat-resistant gloves and their heavy-duty, full-body aprons

emblazoned with the stylish Weber logo. Having said that, I also have a pair of cheap heat-resistant, silicone mittens, which I like to use for flipping meat over or removing hot meat from the smoker. Shop around and buy the best protective gear you can afford—your hands and clothing will thank you for it.

Flavor Chunks, Chips, and Pellets

When using charcoal, electricity, or gas as a heat source, wood of some sort must be added to the mix in order to flavor the meat. This is where wood chunks and wood chips come in. These can be purchased in varying sizes and types of wood almost anywhere smokers or grills are sold. The most common varieties are hickory and mesquite, but other woods such as apple, cherry, oak, and pecan can also be found if you look around a bit. I go into more detail on suitable wood for smoking on pages 19–21. If you cannot find the wood you want where you live, consider looking online at retailers like Amazon.com.

Electric smokers such as the Bradley and the Traeger use compressed sawdust in the form of pellets or biscuits to smoke the meat. These can be purchased in almost any flavor directly from the manufacturer, in specialty stores, or online.

TIPS AND TECHNIQUES
Seasoning a Smoker

All new smokers must be seasoned. Oils, paints, and other chemicals are used during the manufacturing process, leaving residue on the metal. If you don't season your smoker (and thereby remove this residue) your food will taste and smell like something that it shouldn't, and you could be ingesting dangerous substances. You should also season your smoker if you haven't used it in more than two years and after any

general cleaning with soap or chemicals (see Cleaning Your Smoker, below).

To season a smoker, simply spray a light coating of cooking oil on all inside surfaces. Then run the smoker through a normal cooking session, excluding the meat. That is, run it at 225°F using your favorite wood for smoke. This seasoning session should last approximately two hours. The smoker can then be safely used for smoking meat.

Cleaning Your Smoker

There are a few things you can do to keep your smoker clean from one smoking session to the next. As with any cooking device, the grate or cooking surface should be kept very clean. For this reason I recommend using a wad of foil or a grate brush to remove any loose material. You can then run the grate or cooking surface through the dishwasher on the pots and pans cycle. They'll usually come out spotless. If it's been a while since you last cleaned your grates and there are lots of stubborn bits of debris between the rails, you can place them in your oven and run it through a self-clean cycle (assuming the grates will fit in your oven). This ramps the heat in the oven up to about 900°F and burns off the debris. The grates should come out clean and shiny.

TO SOAK OR NOT TO SOAK?

This is probably the question I am asked most frequently when it comes to the use of wood chips or chunks, and the answer comes down to personal need and experience.

My recommendation is to soak the wood only if you absolutely must. I rarely do, simply because it just isn't necessary in most cases. As a caveat to that statement, I have found that I must soak wood chunks for about 30 to 60 minutes when I am using them in my Brinkmann Gourmet Electric Smoker & Grill. In this smoker, you must place the wood chunks on top of the lava rocks between the curved areas of the heating element. If the wood chunks are left dry they will burst into flames within minutes of putting them into the smoker. If you soak them first, you can get 45 to 60 minutes of excellent smoke with no flare-ups.

I recommend deep-cleaning your smoker about once a year. Use a basic degreaser like Simple Green and a nylon scrub brush to remove as much of the grease and muck from the smoker walls as possible. For the more stubborn stuff, you may need to use a plastic putty knife as a scraper. Once everything is sparkling clean again and the inside has been well rinsed to remove all traces of soaps and cleaners, the smoker will need to be re-seasoned (see Seasoning a Smoker, previous page).

Using a Smoker and Grill Together

Many folks who get interested in the method of cooking meat over low heat are previously avid grillers. This can be advantageous, since there are still many uses for the grill while smoke cooking, and experience with higher heat can play a part in producing some really delicious food.

The first application of a grill that comes to mind is finishing off chicken. Whole chickens do very well in the smoker, but the low and slow method of cooking tends to produce rubbery skin. For this reason, I recommend removing chicken from the smoker about 15 minutes before it is finished cooking, and using a hot grill to crispen the skin. This way you get the best of both worlds: slow smoked chicken that is tender and moist with crispy, delicious skin.

You can also use the grill to prepare the vegetables or sides you are serving with the main entrée—a veggie stir-fry, for example, made in a pan or piece of foil with the sides turned up, or tomatoes brushed with olive oil and basil and placed directly on the grate. Some things are just better suited to the grill, and your job is to know what to grill and what to smoke low and slow.

If your grill has a side burner, this is a nifty place to prepare a pot of barbecued beans or to warm up a sauce or marinade to brush onto the meat just before it is finished. There are so many options—you just need to be creative to see how much of the meal you can prepare outdoors. Not only does cooking outside make food taste better; it also keeps the heat out of the kitchen and, better yet, it keeps you out by the smoker where you probably want to be anyway.

Logging Your Smoking Sessions

Everyone who knows me knows that I'm a big fan of keeping notes. If you're anything like me, you'll say to yourself, "Yeah, I'll remember that," but then you don't. The next day that info is long gone, overwritten by other data that is so much more recent and important.

You've also no doubt heard the saying, "If you do what you've always done, you'll get what you've always gotten." Although this saying is often used to motivate people to change, there's also something to be said for consistency. What if what you've done produces a delicious result? How in the world will you repeat that perfect smoking session if you can't remember exactly what you did?

Keep a logbook of cooking temperature, type of wood, weather, how much charcoal you used, how long the cooking session took, etc. This way you can either repeat what you did or change it up a bit based on the given variables. I created a template document for this purpose; I put copies of the template in a three-ring binder and fill in the information while I am cooking.

Your log does not have to be complex; in fact, it can be as simple as jotting some notes on a pad of paper. However you choose to keep notes is up to you, but I do recommend that you do it. I still go back and refer to cooking times and temperatures from smokes I did years ago, especially for things that I don't cook often. These notes have been extremely valuable to me over the years.

Using Pans and Foil in Your Smoker

The most accepted method of smoking meat is to place it right on the grate. This gives the meat excellent exposure to the smoke and creates a nice bark, or firm, tasty crust, on its surface. So why do it any other way? I'm glad you asked.

Smoking meat in foil

It's a technique that's become known as the "Texas crutch," and more and more folks are doing it—wrapping their meat in foil to tenderize it and keep in the moisture. Purist smokers strictly maintain that this is not the correct way to smoke meat, but a lot of people believe that the low and slow method of cooking is more about enjoying the experience.

I must admit that I don't employ the use of foil very often. Call me lazy, or just set in my ways, but I've found I like to leave most things completely exposed on the grate for the entire cooking time.

That said, foil can be a helpful tool when used properly. In my recipe for 3-2-1 Ribs (page 85), where the ribs are placed on the smoker grate for three hours, then wrapped in foil for two hours, then unwrapped and placed back on the grate for a final hour, the ribs are effectively steamed in the foil, which super-tenderizes the meat. These ribs are so fall-off-the-bone tender that a good number of people have become converts to this method.

Since smoke permeates meat more easily when it is uncooked and the pores are open, the smoking process should occur in the first stage of cooking, and the foiling or steaming process in the last stages. For the best results with foil, wrap the meat only after it has reached a fairly high internal temperature of around 165°F.

I must warn you that not all foil is created equal. I recommend purchasing high-quality heavy-duty foil for best results. I have been tempted into buying cheap generic brands of foil on several occasions, and almost without exception, I regretted my decision the first time I tried to cook with them. Generic brands just do not hold up as well as brand-name foils. The extra expense is well worth the lack of aggravation.

Smoking meat in a pan

I sometimes smoke meat in a pan for a couple of reasons. First, it allows me to save the drippings from the meat so I can use it as *jus*. Second, the close proximity of the drippings to the meat seems to produce a juicier and more tender result.

The downside to this method is that while the surface of the meat will be soft and moist and tasty, it will not have that firm crust so many people enjoy. This bothered me at first, but after comparing the advantages and disadvantages of smoking meat on a grate versus in a pan, I've found I prefer the latter for larger cuts like pork shoulder and brisket. Using the pan method for these meats produces a taste and tenderness that are unrivaled. I do recommend rotating the meat from top to bottom every two hours or so for the first half of the cooking session to ensure even smoke permeation.

Smoking Multiple Pieces of Meat

I always feel the need to fill my smoker with meat just so the heat, smoke, and time won't be wasted. Maybe this is my frugal side coming out, or perhaps it's just an excuse to make lots of succulent barbecue, but it just makes sense to me not to waste a grate when it could be the home

Type of meat	Size/weight	Finish time (T)	Required time (R)	Start time (S)
Brisket	10 pounds	8 p.m.	15 hours	5 a.m.
Ribs	One rack	8 p.m.	6 hours	2 p.m.
Chicken	One whole bird	8 p.m.	4 hours	4 p.m.

for another rack of ribs or a nice plump pork butt or brisket.

Multiple pieces of meat will cook in about the same amount of time as one piece. The smoker will take a bit more time to come up to temperature due to the extra cold mass from additional portions of meat, but this will not make much difference to the overall plan as long as you make sure there is ample space for air and smoke to get around the meat. The best thing you can do is to place as much meat as you like in the smoker making sure it is not overly crowded, then limit your lid removals to when they are absolutely necessary.

What about cooking different kinds and cuts of meat at the same time? Why sure! This just takes a little advance planning, because it's all about timing. Start by determining how much time each individual piece will require. If dinnertime is at eight p.m., work backward to determine when each piece of meat will need to be added to the smoker so all pieces are done at the same time.

The table above shows a sample plan for serving a dinner of brisket, ribs, and chicken at eight p.m., assuming an average smoker temperature of 225°F to 240°F. My formula is Finish Time (T) – Required Time (R) = Start Time (S).

It's not really as complicated as it sounds. In order to get all the meat done at the same time, you just have to be organized and look at it in a logical way. Once you do this a few times, you will likely

be able to plan it out without even writing it down. Suddenly it will just start making a lot of sense.

FLAVORING MEAT

Using Rubs, Marinades, Mops, and Sauces

As far back as I can remember, I've always wanted steak sauce on steak, lots of salt and ketchup on french fries, extra salad dressing on my salads . . . you get the idea. I love to add extra flavor to my foods, including when I'm smoking meat. While I want the natural flavor of the cut to come through, I also want a little something to enhance that flavor. This is where rubs, marinades, mops, and sauces come in. All add flavor to smoked meat, though they're applied differently.

Rubs

A rub is a mixture of dried seasonings and spices that is sprinkled on or massaged into meat. A rub can be applied the night before or right before the meat is placed on the smoker. While some folks swear that putting a rub on for several hours prior to smoking is the best, I have not been able to detect a big difference in taste when I apply a rub several hours in advance versus right before the meat goes in the smoker. I prefer to do what's convenient, so sometimes I rub the meat hours ahead of smoking, and other times I do it immediately before.

A rub can consist of any number of dry ingredients, but beware of rubs that have high

salt content; they can cause the end product to be too salty and can even dry out the meat. Rubs can be applied directly to the surface of the meat or used together with a sticking agent, such as yellow mustard, which is put on the meat before the rub is layered on top. The mustard will lose its tangy flavor during the smoking process, but it creates a wonderful crust.

Marinades

A marinade is a liquid mixture of spices, oil, and usually some kind of vinegar, in which meat is soaked to flavor and tenderize it, usually for 12 to 24 hours prior to a smoking session. A marinade can be as quick and simple as a bottle of zesty Italian dressing, or it can be much more complex; some recipes for marinades are a laundry list of flavor-enhancing and meat-tenderizing ingredients. Marinades are also sometimes used to "mop" (see below) the meat while it cooks. This keeps the surface of the meat moist and adds extra flavor.

Mops

A mop is a liquid such as apple juice, apple cider, or even a marinade mixture, which is brushed or sprayed onto the meat while it cooks to keep the surface moist and perhaps to add another layer of flavor.

Some folks say you should not add any liquid to the surface of meat while it cooks. They claim it makes the outside of the meat too soft, does not actually add any flavor, and causes you to open the lid or door of your smoker way too often, thereby losing valuable heat and potentially increasing the cooking time.

I can say that I have tried it both ways—mopping versus just leaving the meat alone while it smokes—and there are times when mopping makes a difference and times when it does not. I don't like it when the outside of chicken or ribs dries out while they cook, so I mop them at least a few times while they are smoking to keep the surface of the meat moist. For things like brisket and pork shoulder, I usually don't bother; the fat on the outside of the meat does the basting for me as it renders.

Sauces

Barbecue sauces vary widely depending on where you live. In the Midwest and farther south into some parts of Texas, barbecue sauce is ketchup-based and is usually both sweet and spicy. In South Carolina, barbecue sauce is mustard-based. Alabama has a mayonnaise-based white sauce that is out of this world. And then there's the vinegar-based sauce you'll find in North Carolina, which I grew up on. And that's just the beginning of the wonderful but diverse world of barbecue sauces.

Barbecue sauce is usually applied at the end of the smoking process, about 30 minutes before the meat is done cooking or at the table. My favorite way to serve barbecue sauce is in individual condiment cups right at the table so my friends and family can help themselves if they like.

Injecting

Who would have thought that using a large injector to push marinades and other liquids into the center of meat would become a fad, but it seems that everyone is doing it these days. Many competitive smoking teams claim that their special marinade, injected into the meat, is the secret behind their winning streaks. I started experimenting with this only in the last few years, and while I don't always inject my meat, I have become a huge proponent of this process. I think you will too if you take the time to try it.

But what kinds of meat can you inject? I love to inject butter and other seasonings into our Thanksgiving turkey before placing it on the smoker; the resulting flavor is nothing short of amazing. I make another tasty treat by combining equal parts of wing sauce and my favorite barbecue sauce and injecting the mix into chicken drumsticks for monster wings. You've never tasted anything so delicious—that's a promise! I also inject white chocolate ganache into chocolate cake (page 200) for that died-and-gone-to-heaven effect.

Almost anything can be injected into meat. I like to start with melted butter or olive oil and then I add ingredients depending on what type of meat and style of dish I am cooking. If you're not the creative type, your local supermarket likely has a wonderful selection of injectable marinades (like the ones made by Cajun Injector) that will add some excellent flavor. You can also use most meat marinades as injections. Another fine example of an injection is my mop water (page 157), which is basically melted butter, water, and Cajun seasoning; this works as well on the inside as it does on the outside.

Some of you may be saying, "This sounds like something I'd like to try, but where do I get

one of these injectors?" Many of the injectable marinades sold in supermarkets come packaged with an injector. You can also find several different types of injectors in the cooking utensil aisle of department stores, or online at Amazon.com. Most are similar in size and in the way they work, and in many cases the needles are interchangeable.

Brining

Brining is the method of immersing meat in a saltwater solution to increase its capacity to hold moisture. The scientific explanation is much more involved, but in layman's terms, liquid is drawn into the fibers and cells of the meat during brining via the process of osmosis. The extra moisture helps to combat the drying that naturally takes place when meat is subjected to heat, and

Brining poultry using no-heat method

the result is a juicier entrée. Even brined meat that is slightly overcooked will stay juicy and moist. An added bonus to brining is that any flavors added to the water—sugar, soy sauce, beer, or juice, for example—will also be pulled into the meat. I generally brine poultry and fish only, but lots of folks brine other meats, so don't be afraid to experiment.

Brining is very easy and does absolute wonders for meat, but it does require some planning. The most basic ingredients are water and kosher salt (use a ratio of 1 gallon of water to 1 cup of kosher salt), but you will probably want to add other things for added flavor. My own recipes, which are the ones I use most often, are on pages 153 to 155.

Note that most brine recipes will call for a certain amount of water with a certain amount of salt and then the other ingredients. If you want to experiment with your own recipes, make sure to keep to the recommended ratio of 1 gallon of liquid to 1 cup of salt. You can substitute things like apple juice for some of the water if you're using a large amount (such as a cup or more). However, ingredients like soy sauce, Worcestershire sauce, lemon juice, and hot sauce, which are added in smaller amounts, should be

in addition to the water and not replacements.

Be sure to use kosher salt in your brine solutions, since it dissolves in water more readily than most other types of salt.

Making brine
No-heat Method
This method does not require heat, and should be used only when you are keeping the brine basic and are not adding any spices or sugar, which would require heat to dissolve or bring out the oils and/or flavors in the ingredients.

1. Fill a large container, such as a 1-gallon tea pitcher, with ½ gallon of water.
2. Add ½ cup of kosher salt and stir until it is completely dissolved and the water is clear.
3. If you wish, add other basic ingredients to this solution, such as low-sodium soy sauce, Worcestershire sauce, hot sauce, lemon juice, apple cider, beer, etc.

When using this basic method, I make only ½-gallon batches of brine at one time, since I almost always use a 1-gallon tea pitcher and the smaller volume allows me to add the other ingredients and still have plenty of room to stir the brine without most of it ending up on the counter. If you have and want to use a really large

container or bowl that will handle a full gallon of water plus ingredients, go for it.

Heat Method

1. Place 1 gallon of water in a large stockpot set over medium-high heat. (You can actually use as little as a ½ gallon of water, but if the salt added in the next step doesn't dissolve completely, the water has reached its maximum salt concentration value and you will need to add more water. Do not exceed a total of 1 gallon of water.)
2. Add 1 cup of kosher salt and stir until it is completely dissolved and the water is clear.
3. Add other ingredients such as pepper, cloves, rosemary, crushed red pepper, brown sugar, etc., and allow the brine to come to a slow boil.
4. Turn the heat down to low and allow the brine to simmer for about 15 minutes.
5. Remove from heat and let the brine cool for a few minutes before placing it in the refrigerator.

Setting the bird or fish in the brine

The brine solution *must* cool down to a temperature of 33°F to 39°F before you pour it over the meat. This is crucial to keep the meat safe from spoilage. Once the brine is in the 33°F

BRINING BASICS

When brining, follow these three simple rules to turn out poultry that is safe and delicious to eat.

- Don't brine in a reactive container; be sure to use glass or food-grade plastic.
- Ensure the brine is at a temperature of 33°F to 39°F before submerging the meat in it, and maintain that temperature range during the entire brining process.
- Never reuse the brine; it must be thrown out when finished.

Also keep in mind that brined meats tend to cook a little faster, so watch your bird closely toward the end of the cooking process.

to 39°F range, pour it along with any remaining water from your initial 1 gallon into a nonreactive container such as an ice chest, a large Tupperware bowl, or a 1- to 2-gallon Ziploc bag—anything that is clean and made of glass or food-grade plastic and is large enough to cover the meat you are brining will work great. It's always a good idea to make enough brine to cover the meat completely rather than having to stop and make another batch. I like to make a little extra just to be sure, but you'll have to use your own judgment. I have found that 2 gallons is plenty of brine for

a 12-pound turkey when using a 5-gallon plastic bucket.

A chicken or turkey will tend to float to the top of the brine. To keep the bird completely submerged in the water, I place a heavy plate on top of it. You can also put a clean brick into a gallon-sized Ziploc bag and place it on the bird. Either way, the poultry must be completely covered with the brine.

Food-grade plastic

When brining, it is very important to use only glass or plastic containers made of food-grade plastic. It can be difficult to determine if a container is food grade or not, so the best option is to use a plastic container marked for handling food, such as a Tupperware bowl or a bucket from a restaurant or food-service establishment that previously contained sauce, oil, or other edible items.

How long should you brine?

Different sizes of bird need to be brined for different amounts of time. For instance, a whole chicken will require only about three to four

hours, while a 12-pound turkey will need to brine overnight or from 10 to 12 hours for best results. Turkey legs will do just fine with about two hours of brining.

THE SMOKING MEAT PANTRY

Several folks have asked me over the years which spices, condiments, and other ingredients they should keep on hand so they can smoke meat when the urge arises. This is very personal and should be tailored to your own needs and tastes, but I have provided some guidelines to make sure you are well stocked.

Must-Have Dried Spices

Here is my dream spice rack. It would be ideal to have each of these in stock and organized in alphabetical order so the one you want is easy to find. This isn't an exhaustive list, but these are the items I could do almost anything with.

Allspice, ground	Kosher salt
Aniseed	Lemon peel
Arrowroot powder	Mace
Basil leaves	Marjoram leaves
Bay leaves	Mustard powder
Black pepper	Mustard seed
Caraway seed	Nutmeg, ground
Cardamom, ground	Onion powder
Cardamom seed	Onion salt
Cayenne pepper	Orange peel
Celery seed	Oregano, ground
Chervil	Paprika
Chili powder	Parsley
Chopped chives	Peppermint leaves
Cinnamon, ground	Pickling spice
Cinnamon sticks	Poppy seed
Cloves, ground	Poultry seasoning
Cloves, whole	Red pepper flakes
Coriander, ground	Rosemary leaves
Coriander seed	Saffron
Cream of tartar	Sage, rubbed
Cumin, ground	Sesame seed
Curry powder	Spearmint leaves
Dill seed	Tarragon leaves
Fennel seed	Thyme, ground
Garlic powder	Thyme leaves
Garlic salt	Turmeric
Ginger, ground	White pepper
Italian seasoning	

Apple juice	Lemon juice
Beef broth	Mustard
Brown sugar	Ready-to-use injectable
Chicken broth	marinades (such as
Curing salt (such as	Cajun Injector brand)
Morton Tender Quick)	Soy sauce
Extra virgin olive oil	Sriracha sauce
Frank's RedHot Original	Tabasco sauce
Cayenne Pepper Sauce	Turbinado sugar
Ketchup	Worcestershire sauce

Other Useful Pantry Items

Here is a list of condiments, sauces, and miscellaneous dry ingredients—some of which need refrigeration—that are also useful pantry items. They add so much flavor to the smoking recipes I like to throw together at a moment's notice.

FOOD SAFETY

When you're feeding family, friends, and other guests, you have a responsibility to follow certain safety protocols in the processing and cooking of food. This topic is especially near and dear to my heart simply because I would be devastated if anyone ever got sick from something I prepared, especially if it was preventable.

You must follow a few simple rules when cooking meat at a low temperature. Luckily, the United States Department of Agriculture (USDA) provides all the information we need to avoid foodborne pathogens such as E. coli (*Escherichia coli*) and salmonella.

Buy from Reputable Sources

Make sure you purchase your meats from reliable businesses that follow safety protocols during butchering and processing. This can be difficult to ensure if you buy meat from a grocery store or meat market, so it is imperative to get to know the butcher or meat-handling personnel. When you foster those relationships, you will gain some valuable knowledge about the origin of the meat you are buying and how it is handled prior to your purchase.

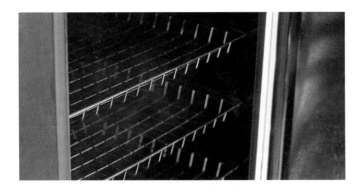

Always thaw meat in the refrigerator and *never* at room temperature. Make sure meat is completely thawed before smoking it. This is important for two reasons:

- Thawed meat cooks more evenly.
- Thawed meat is in the danger zone of 40°F to 140°F—that precarious range in which bad bacteria and foodborne pathogens seem to thrive—for less time than if the meat is partially frozen when you start cooking it.

Meat should be prepared and cooked so as to minimize the amount of time it stays in the danger zone. It is also important to check your refrigerator periodically to make sure it is maintaining a temperature of 33°F to 39°F.

I recently went into a local grocery store and noticed that there was no hand sanitizer anywhere near the meat-packaging station. I asked the butcher about it, but all I got was the classic deer-in-the-headlights look. I proceeded to ask a few other people, but all gave the same look. No one knew where the sanitizer was or if they even had any in the store. I'm not talking about a small backwoods grocery store here; this was a retailer whose name everyone would recognize. I e-mailed the corporate office, explaining that this was unsanitary and that I fully expected to see hand sanitizer stations set up not only for the customers but for the employees behind the counter as well. After all, this is common practice when it comes to cleanliness and food safety.

In fewer than 24 hours I received an e-mail reply from someone in the PR department letting me know that this would be taken care of immediately and that I could contact them again if I had any further concerns. I returned to the store a few days later, and lo and behold there were hand sanitizer stations in several prominent locations behind the counter and next to the meat displays. It took a little effort on my part, but I feel like I made a difference not only in the safety of my family but in the safety and well-being of countless others who regularly shop at this store. After all, a pound of prevention is worth an ounce of cure, and when it comes to food safety, you can never take too many precautions.

Keep Meat Cool
On the road

Once you have purchased your meat, you need to bring it home. Take special precautions to make sure it stays cold during the trip, especially in the summer. To get from the store to my home is usually about a 15-minute drive, so I don't worry about it. But if you take more than 30 minutes to get home, find a way to keep the meat cool. If you are driving, it would be very smart to keep an ice chest in your vehicle with a single bag of ice. Place the meat in the ice chest and put the bag of ice on top for the trip home. Ice is cheap and you can rest assured that the meat will stay at a safe temperature until you get home. If you aren't shopping with a car, consider bringing an insulated bag and a small ice pack to keep the meat cool.

Here's a summary of what you should and shouldn't do to ensure your food is completely safe.

Chill

- Keep meat as cool as possible while traveling from the store to your home.
- Keep meat refrigerated, and ensure your refrigerator is maintaining a proper temperature of 33°F to 39°F.
- Thaw frozen meat in the refrigerator, *not* on the counter.
- Make sure meat is completely thawed before smoking it.
- Minimize the time that meat is out of the refrigerator when preparing it for smoking. (Allowing it to sit on the counter for 30 minutes prior to smoking is a good practice to avoid creosote, but any longer than this opens the door to bacteria.)

Clean

- Wash hands with soap and hot water often while handling and preparing meat.
- Wash all surfaces, dishes, utensils, and tools that have been in contact with raw meat with hot, soapy water.
- Never reuse plastic bags that have been used to transfer or store raw meat.

Separate

- Use separate designated cutting boards for meats and vegetables.
- Use clean dishes and utensils for removing meat from the smoker.

Cook

- Smoke meat at or above 225°F.
- Refrigerate meat within two hours of removal from smoker.
- Ensure meats are cooked to my recommended safety temperatures (below).
- Use a calibrated and tested thermometer to check meat for proper doneness.

At home

Be sure to put meat in the refrigerator or freezer as soon as you arrive home. It's a good idea to make space in the refrigerator before you go shopping to ensure you can place the meat in it right away. To ensure meat doesn't spoil before its expiration date, it must be kept below 40°F. I highly recommend using a thermometer in your refrigerator to ensure that this is actually the case instead of assuming that your nice shiny appliance is doing its job. Commercial refrigerators require this, but it is a good thing to do at home as well.

When you take meat out of the refrigerator to prepare it for smoking, you should process it quickly. Allowing meat to sit on the counter for 30 minutes prior to smoking is a good practice to avoid creosote, but if further delay occurs, put the meat back in the refrigerator.

Avoid Cross-Contamination

Cross-contamination occurs when foodborne pathogens from one item are transferred to another. This occurs when raw or undercooked meat comes into contact with food that is ready to be eaten. Wash your hands often with soap and hot water while handling and preparing meat, and place dishes, utensils, and other tools used in the preparation of raw meat into hot, soapy water immediately after use to make sure they are properly cleaned and sanitized. Be sure to use clean plates, utensils, and tools for removing and serving meat from the smoker.

Cook Meat at a Safe Temperature

Once you place the meat on the grate of the

to come back soon, your wallet suffers.

So how do you figure out how much is enough? Well, it's not an exact science. There are formulas out there, but I just don't think a pound of meat per person fits every scenario. For example, men eat more than women, older folks eat less than middle-aged folks, young children don't usually eat that much, and teenaged boys are garbage disposals with legs, able to eat enormous amounts of food. Quantity also depends on how the food is being served. If hot wings are the only thing on offer, I can eat at least a dozen, if not two dozen before I land the plane and call it a night. But if the wings are served with bread, baked beans, potato salad, and possibly other sides, then I might eat half a dozen at the most.

Bottom line: the better you know the demographics of your get-together, the better you can plan. Estimate the number of men, women, and children at the very least. Any more details will just help you further.

For a main entrée, I generally plan on about 1½ pounds for men and teen boys; 1 pound for women, teen girls, and seniors; and ½ pound for children. This formula works out for me in almost every case, with a little left over—but it is based on averages and does not work if you're serving the meal buffet-style. For buffets, adjust the amounts upward, because people tend to pile up their plates. When serving meat as an appetizer, I cut the total amount by about half.

I have a phobia about running out of food, so I tend to overcompensate. It's nothing for me to throw on an extra brisket just to make myself feel better. Most of the time, though, I find that the math works and that I should plan the meal using the facts.

smoker and the lid is closed, the smoke will naturally retard the growth of bacteria. However, the USDA recommends that meat be cooked at 225°F or above to ensure it does not stay in the danger zone longer than necessary. I recommend cooking at the lower temperatures of 225°F to 240°F for the true smoking experience.

EATING AND ENJOYING SMOKED MEAT
How Much Is Enough?

This is the age-old question that many folks ask when they are about to have a party or get-together. You don't want to run out—that would be a disaster—but neither do you want to blow the budget and have a ton of food left over. Although sending guests home with doggie bags would make them extremely happy and only too eager

Keeping Smoked Meat Warm

Dinner is at eight p.m. and it's only five-thirty. You notice that the brisket is already creeping up on 195°F, and since the dinner guests will not be arriving for another two hours, what in the world can you do to keep the meat warm without drying it out or cooking it further? There is a simple solution, and it involves heavy-duty foil, towels, and an empty ice chest.

Wrap the meat in a double layer of heavy-duty foil, making sure the shiny side faces in. Air gets trapped between the layers and creates an insulating effect. The heat also reflects off of the shiny foil on the inside of the package, thereby staying inside with the meat instead of leaking out.

Place the package in a deep pan just in case there are any leaks. Wrap the package and pan in a thick towel and place it in an empty ice chest lined with another heavy towel folded in half. Fill the remaining space above the pan of meat with more towels, pillows, or a small blanket if necessary.

The meat will stay above 140°F for up to four hours in this state, and will be juicier and more tender when you take it out than when you put it in. I have been known to do this on purpose for that very reason.

Transporting and Reheating Techniques

I receive many e-mails, especially around the holidays, from folks asking me how to cook a turkey or other meat at home and then transport it to Grandma's house. I will tell you right up front that the best way to eat smoked meat is right out of the smoker (or within four hours if kept warm using the method described above). It tends to lose that certain something when it is reheated. But sometimes reheating is necessary, so here are my recommendations for making the best of a not-so-ideal situation.

Vacuum pack

The best method for preparing smoked meat for reheating later is to slice, chop, or pull the meat, then pack it into 1- to 2-pound vacuum packs. I am a big fan of vacuum packing at home. The equipment on the market these days is easy to use and fairly affordable.

To reheat the vacuum-packaged meat, bring a pot of water to boiling, then turn off the heat. Drop the packages in the hot water for 12 to 18 minutes to reheat to a perfect eating temperature.

Slow cooker

The second method requires a slow cooker. First, slice or pull the meat immediately after it has finished smoking and has rested for the prescribed time; save the meat's drippings as *jus* for the reheating process. Place the meat in the removable part of the slow cooker and cover it with foil or plastic wrap before putting the lid on. This container can be placed in the refrigerator for up to three days.

To reheat, remove the foil or plastic wrap from the meat and pour some of the saved *jus* or some broth over the top. Set the removable pot back into the slow cooker base and heat on high for three to four hours, or until the meat is warm enough to serve.

Oven

Using the oven is the best method for reheating quickly when you do not have a vacuum sealer. After the meat has finished smoking, place it in a deep pan covered with foil and refrigerate until you are ready to reheat it (not to exceed three days). Save the meat's drippings as *jus* for the reheating process.

To reheat, preheat the oven to 350°F. Remove the foil from the meat, and pour some of the saved

jus or some broth over the top. Recover with foil and set in the oven for 30 to 45 minutes, or until the meat reaches the desired serving temperature.

COLD SMOKING BASICS

An entire book could be devoted to cold smoking, so while I don't intend to delve too deeply into this topic here, I can give a few pointers on how to set up your smoker for creating smoke with little or no residual heat.

Cold smoking is great for cheese, bacon, seafood, and lean meats such as steak or wild game. For the last three items, which are typically grilled, I recommend cold smoking for 30 to 45 minutes right before grilling. Although they would be exposed to smoke from grilling only, the smoke flavor would be minimal because of the short duration spent on the grill. By adding a cold smoking session just before grilling, the smoke flavor can be greatly enhanced.

For cheese especially, it is imperative that the heat be no higher than 90°F to prevent the cheese from melting all over your smoker. There are several options for creating the much-needed smoke while keeping the heat to the bare minimum.

Dual Smoker Method

This method of cold smoking is the most difficult. I mention it because it has been used so much over the years, but I don't recommend it since there are much easier ways to accomplish the task.

Basically, smoker A is filled with lit charcoal and some wood chips or chunks to create smoke. A dryer hose or other pipe is attached to the top of smoker A and run slightly uphill about 6 to 10 feet to smoker B. The hose is attached to the bottom of smoker B, which contains the cheese or other food you want to smoke. As the smoke travels from smoker A to smoker B, it cools down and does not increase the temperature in smoker B beyond 90°F.

Soldering Iron Method

Fill a large metal coffee can with a mix of wood chips and wood chunks. Plug a soldering iron into a wall outlet and insert the end into the coffee can. Place the cheese or meat on the top grate of your smoker or grill, and the smoking apparatus on the bottom grate or in the firebox, and let the magic happen. The can will need to be shaken occasionally to knock down ash,

but it will create smoke with minimal heat production.

Three Hot Coals and a Wood Chunk

I know it sounds like a nursery rhyme, but this is actually a simple way to cold smoke. Place the cheese or meat on the grate of your smoker. Set three lit charcoal briquettes flat in the charcoal pan or firebox of your smoker. Place a flat wood chunk on top of the charcoal to create smoke. Provide a little airflow and replace the charcoal and/or wood chunk as needed to keep the smoke going for the desired period of time.

Smoke Generators

Devices designed to create smoke and turn any smoker or grill into a cold smoker can also be purchased. They are inexpensive and are recommended for real hassle-free cold smoking. The two devices I have used extensively are the Smoke Daddy and the A-Maze-N-Smoker, both of which do a wonderful job.

Smoke Daddy

The Smoke Daddy is a cylinder that attaches easily to your current grill or smoker via a ¾-inch

hole using a washer and a nut. The cylinder is filled with wood chips or pellets and is lit with a butane torch to provide smoke. A fish-tank air pump attached to the cylinder provides positive pressure to push the smoke into the grill or smoker. It works for several hours at a time and can be easily refilled on the fly for extended cold smoking sessions. Visit www.smokedaddyinc.com for more information on this product.

A-Maze-N-Smoker

This small, 6-inch-square device looks like a maze and uses very fine wood dust lit at one or both ends to create smoke. Once lit, the wood dust smolders from one end of the maze to the other, creating smoke for up to six hours if lit at one end and up to three hours if lit at both ends (though more smoke is produced in the latter scenario). It's very simple to use, can be washed in the dishwasher, and can be used for cold smoking in any smoker or grill. They also have a new model that uses pellets (instead of wood dust), which produce more smoke and burn for up to 11 hours unattended. More information on this product can be found at www.amazenproducts.com.

MASTER TABLE OF SMOKING TIMES AND TEMPERATURES

	Smoking temperature	Finished temperature	Estimated cook time	Notes
Poultry				
Chicken breasts, boneless, skinless	225°F to 240°F	165°F	2½ hours	Use bacon on top to keep the meat moist
Chicken quarters	225°F to 240°F	165°F	4 hours	Higher temperature helps crispen the skin
Chicken thighs/legs	225°F to 240°F	165°F	3 hours	Higher temperature helps crispen the skin
Chicken, whole (4 lb)	225°F to 240°F	165°F	3 to 4 hours	Higher temperature helps crispen the skin
Chicken wings/ drumettes	225°F to 240°F	165°F	2 hours	
Cornish game hen	225°F to 240°F	165°F	4 hours	
Duck, whole	225°F to 240°F	165°F	4 hours	
Turkey breast, bone in	225°F to 240°F	165°F	4 to 6 hours	
Turkey breast, boneless, skinless	225°F to 240°F	165°F	3 to 4 hours	Cover with cheesecloth to keep moist
Turkey legs	225°F to 240°F	165°F	4 hours	
Turkey, whole (12 lb)	225°F to 240°F	165°F	6½ hours	
Pork				
Baby back ribs	225°F to 240°F	N/A	5 hours	Smoke cook until tender
Picnic	225°F to 240°F	205°F	1½ hours per lb	
Pork butt	225°F to 240°F	205°F	1½ hours per lb	
Pork loin	225°F to 240°F	160°F	4 hours	
Spare ribs	225°F to 240°F	N/A	6 hours	Smoke cook until tender
Beef				
Arm chuck roast	225°F to 240°F	180°F	1½ hours per lb	
Back ribs	225°F to 240°F	N/A	5 hours	Smoke cook until tender
Brisket	225°F to 240°F	195°F	1½ hours per lb	
Meatloaf	225°F to 250°F	160°F	3 hours	

	Smoking temperature	Finished temperature	Estimated cook time	Notes
Beef (continued)				
Prime rib, medium-rare	225°F to 240°F	135°F	4 hours	Remove from smoker at 130°F for best results
Tenderloin, medium-rare	250°F to 275°F	130°F	45 minutes per lb	
Fish and seafood				
Mahi-mahi fillet	210°F to 225°F	145°F	2 hours	
Prawns	180°F to 200°F	N/A	1 hour	Cook until shell turns amber/pink
Salmon fillet	150°F to 160°F	145°F	4 to 5 hours	150°F for 2 hours, then 160°F to finish; time depends on size of fillet
Trout, whole	210°F to 225°F	145°F	2 hours	
Specialty				
Bacon-wrapped stuffed jalapeño peppers	225°F to 240°F	N/A	3 hours	
Bacon-wrapped stuffed sausage fatty	225°F to 240°F	N/A	3 hours	
Boudin	225°F to 240°F	N/A	3 hours	
Bratwurst	225°F to 240°F	N/A	2 hours	
Frog legs	225°F to 240°F	N/A	2 hours	
Moink balls	225°F to 240°F	N/A	2 hours	
Vegetables				
Asparagus	225°F to 240°F	N/A	1 hour	Serve crisp; do not overcook
Corn on the cob	225°F to 240°F	N/A	1½ hours	
Potatoes	225°F to 240°F	N/A	3 hours	Cook until soft

(CONTINUED NEXT PAGE)

	Smoking temperature	Finished temperature	Estimated cook time	Notes
Desserts				
Apple pie	275°F	N/A	1½ to 3 hours	
Bananas	200°F	N/A	1 hour	
Peaches	250°F	N/A	30 minutes	
Cheese				
Cheddar	Less than 90°F	N/A	4 hours	
Cheese sticks	Less than 90°F	N/A	1 hour	
Cream cheese	75°F to 80°F	N/A	2 hours	

SMOKING LINGO AND TERMS

ABT (ATOMIC BUFFALO TURD) A jalapeño pepper stuffed with cream cheese and any number of other ingredients, such as meat, cheddar cheese, and onions, then wrapped in bacon and smoked for three hours or until the bacon is crispy.

CHIMNEY (OR STACK) The round (or square in some cases) tube-like device coming out of the smoke chamber that allows smoke to escape from the smoker.

DAMPER The vent in a smoker that allows air to enter and escape, thereby affecting the airflow within the smoker.

FATTY A chub of breakfast sausage rolled flat, stuffed with cheese, vegetables, and other ingredients, rolled back up, and wrapped with a weave of bacon. This roll is smoked for about three hours or until the sausage is cooked and the bacon is crispy.

FIREBOX The area of the smoker where the fire is built. This is most generally found on horizontal offset smokers.

INTAKE The damper on or near the firebox that can be adjusted by the user to allow more or less air into the firebox. More air equals a hotter fire; less air equals a cooler fire.

LOW AND SLOW A term used to describe the low heat and slow cooking method used to produce tender, juicy, and flavorful food in a smoker or other indirect cooking device.

NAKED A term used to describe ribs that are served with no sauce on them. Most naked ribs are coated with a dry rub prior to smoking, and are served with sauce on the side. (The next time

you're in your favorite "Q" joint, order ribs and ask to have them served "naked." Hopefully you'll get ribs with no sauce instead of wet ribs served by a naked waiter or waitress!)

PITMASTER A person who is highly skilled in the art of using a pit or a smoker to produce perfectly prepared and barbecued meat or other foods.

RAIN CAP A cap on the top of the chimney that can be opened or closed in varying degrees to allow more or less smoke to escape. It's aptly named because it also keeps rain out of the smoker.

RIB RUB A concoction of spices made especially for ribs to flavor them and/or complement the sauce. Most rib rubs also work great on other meats, such as pork shoulder and brisket.

SMOKE CHAMBER (or COOKING CHAMBER) The large bottom chamber in a horizontal offset

smoker. This is the area where the smoke and heat do their job of smoke cooking the meat.

TBS (THIN BLUE SMOKE) A term used to describe what proper smoke looks like. It should be very thin and so pale that it almost has a bluish tint to it. This is the type of smoke that produces the best and cleanest flavor.

WATER PAN A pan for holding water in some smokers, particularly the bullet models. The steam released by the water as it heats helps to regulate the temperature of the smoker.

WET A term that normally applies to ribs when they are basted with sauce or marinade during smoking.

TIPS FOR SMOKING POULTRY

BRINING

I highly recommend that chicken and turkey be brined before smoking. Follow the instructions for brining on pages 37–40 for the best results.

CRISPING THE SKIN

So you like crispy poultry skin but have noticed that smoking chicken or turkey tends to produce rubbery, thick skin that is pretty much inedible? Poultry skin needs high heat to get crispy, but low and slow is where the flavor happens, so you have to find a balance between these two worlds.

To crispen the skin on a chicken or turkey, simply smoke it until the internal temperature of the bird reaches 145°F. Transfer the bird to a hot grill preheated to 350°F to 375°F, and finish it off to 165°F.

You can also smoke cook the bird at 275°F to 300°F to obtain crispy skin, but the cooking time will be much shorter than what is listed in the recipes that follow. This method really cuts the time a bird spends in the smoker, and for me that translates to cutting flavor. I recommend you try several different ways to crispen poultry skin to see what works best for you.

1

POULTRY

REMOVING THE SKIN

It is fairly uncommon to remove poultry skin, but if you desire to do so, wait until your bird is finished smoking. The skin protects the meat as it cooks, while still allowing plenty of smoke to get through. Furthermore, even if you burn the skin, the meat will, in most cases, still be very good. Once a bird is cooked, the skin can easily be removed and discarded if that is your wish.

DEALING WITH THE NECK AND GIBLETS

You will want to remove extra parts from the cavity of the poultry before making any of these recipes. The neck and giblets are not necessary in most cases and can be discarded. If you are planning to use these parts in a different recipe such as gravy or dressing, place them in the refrigerator or freezer for safekeeping.

SMOKED WHOLE CHICKEN

*Chicken is one of the easiest meats to smoke, immensely delicious, and a
good meat to hone your smoking skills on. If it doesn't turn out the way
you want, your loss is fairly negligible in terms of cost and time (compared
to more expensive and time-consuming items like brisket or pork butt).*

RECOMMENDED WOOD Pecan and
mesquite at a 50:50 ratio
ESTIMATED COOK TIME 3 to 4 hours
SERVES 8

2 whole chickens (about 4 lb each)
⅓ cup All-Purpose Rub (page 146)
¼ cup yellow mustard

PREPARATION Brine the chickens, if desired (see pages 37–40).

Rinse the chickens in cold water, making sure also to rinse
the cavities thoroughly. Pull the skin up as much as possible
without tearing it, and use your fingers to push about 1 Tbsp of
the rub under the skin of each chicken so the rub is in direct
contact with the meat.

Apply a thin layer of the mustard to the outside of each
chicken, then pour half (2 Tbsp) of the remaining rub on each
bird and massage it in. The rub will mix with the mustard
and will leave a really nice crust on the outside of the chicken.
Leave the chicken on the counter to bring it up to room
temperature while you set up your smoker.

SMOKING Prepare your smoker for cooking at 225°F to 240°F.
If you are using a charcoal, an electric, or a gas smoker, you
will need enough wood chips or chunks to produce smoke for
at least two hours (three hours for a really smoky flavor).

Place the chickens on the smoker grate breast side down for
the first hour, then flip them breast side up for the remaining
two to three hours. If parts of the chicken, such as the wings,
start to brown too quickly, cover them with small pieces of foil
to prevent further browning.

Insert a digital probe meat thermometer into the thickest
part of a breast or thigh once the chicken has cooked for
about two hours. Inserting a thermometer into the meat too
late in the game will result in unnecessary loss of valuable
juices. The chicken is safe to eat when the thermometer reads
at least 165°F.

When the chicken is finished cooking, remove it from the
smoker and allow it to rest for 20 minutes before carving. If
you want to crispen the skin, see my tip on page 52.

SMOKED BEER CAN CHICKEN

*Traditionally, beer can chicken is a grilling or tailgating
food, and is cooked fast and furious. But smokers can get excellent
results, too. The liquid in the can steams the inside of the chicken
and helps to create a tenderer and tastier bird. Be adventurous in your
choice of beverage—see if you can taste the difference between,
say, beer, orange pop, or Dr Pepper.*

RECOMMENDED WOOD Pecan and
apple at a 50:50 ratio

ESTIMATED COOK TIME 3 to 4 hours

SERVES 4

1 Tbsp coarsely ground black pepper

1 Tbsp kosher salt

1 tsp garlic flakes

1 tsp cayenne pepper

½ tsp dried rosemary leaves

½ tsp dried thyme leaves

1 whole chicken (about 4 lb)

Extra virgin olive oil

12 oz can beer (or soft drink or
fruit juice)

PREPARATION Brine the chicken, if desired (see pages 37–40).

Mix the dry ingredients in a small bowl and set aside. Rub the chicken all over with the olive oil, then sprinkle the dry rub mixture evenly over the outside of the chicken. For added flavor, try to get some of the rub under the skin of the chicken wherever possible.

Leave the chicken on the counter to allow the rub to start working its magic on the meat while you set up your smoker.

SMOKING Prepare the smoker for cooking at 225°F to 240°F. If you are using a charcoal, an electric, or a gas smoker, be sure to have enough wood chips or chunks on hand to keep the smoke going for at least two to three hours.

Once the smoker is ready, open the can of beer or other liquid and empty out about half of the contents. Place the open can on the smoker grate and fit the chicken on top of the can so that the can is partially inside the cavity of the bird. The can will hold the chicken upright and the liquid will steam flavor into the chicken, making it even more moist and delicious.

Insert a digital probe meat thermometer into the thickest part of a breast or thigh once the chicken has cooked for about two hours. Smoke cook the chicken another one to two hours, or until the internal temperature reaches 165°F.

Remove the chicken from the grate, discard the can and its contents, and let the bird rest for 20 to 30 minutes before serving. If you want to crispen the skin, see my tip on page 52. The can does not need to be removed until the chicken is ready to serve.

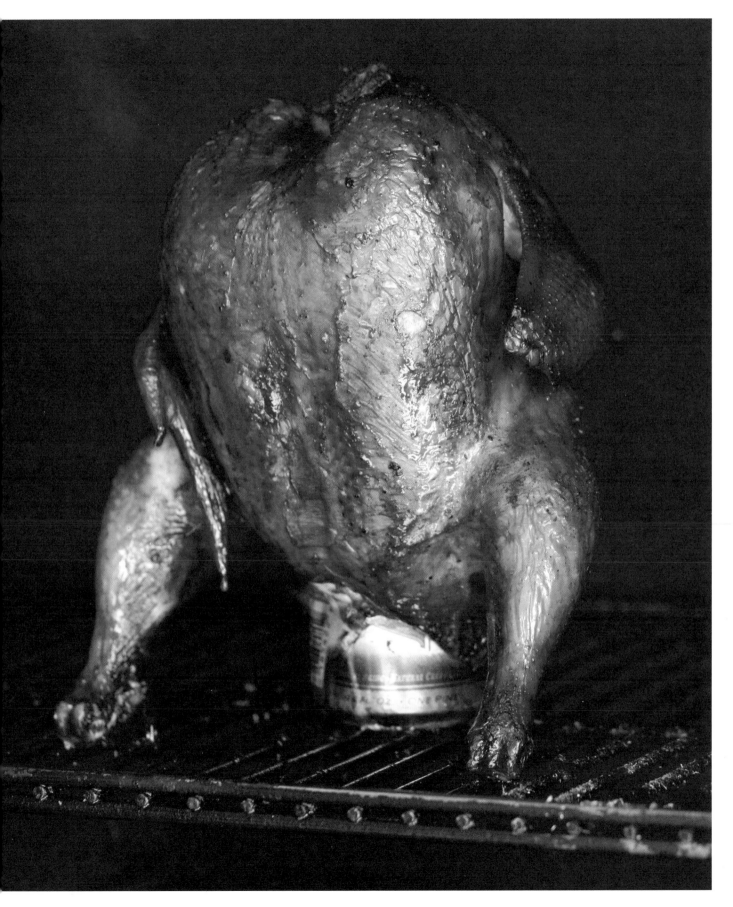

SMOKED CHICKEN QUARTERS

*Chicken quarters are undoubtedly my favorite; in my opinion,
the leg and thigh are the most flavorful parts of the bird, and
there's no need to fight for the breast or wing—coming from a rather
large family has taught me everything about that!*

RECOMMENDED WOOD Pecan and
  apple at a 50:50 ratio

ESTIMATED COOK TIME 4 hours

SERVES 6

---

6 chicken quarters

2 Tbsp yellow mustard

⅓ cup All-Purpose Rub (page 146)
  (or 3 Tbsp lemon pepper)

PREPARATION Brine the chicken quarters, if desired (see pages 37–40).

Rinse the chicken with cold water and pat dry with paper towels. Apply a light layer (1 tsp) of the mustard to each of the quarters, then sprinkle each piece with about 1 Tbsp of the All-Purpose Rub or ½ Tbsp of lemon pepper. Try to get some of the rub under the skin wherever possible, as this will help flavor the meat instead of just the skin. You will find certain areas where the skin is loose enough to pull up. Rub can be placed into these openings and spread with a single finger. Leave the chicken on the counter for about 30 to 45 minutes to bring it up to room temperature and allow the rub to marinate the meat a little while you get your smoker ready.

SMOKING Prepare your smoker for cooking at 225°F to 240°F. If you are using a charcoal, an electric, or a gas smoker, make sure to have enough smoking wood to last about two hours.

Once your smoker is ready, place the chicken quarters directly on the grate with about 1 inch between each piece to allow maximum exposure to the smoke. Insert a digital probe meat thermometer into one of the quarters when they are first placed in the smoker.

Smoke the chicken quarters for four hours or until they reach 165°F in the thickest part of the leg or thigh. To crispen the skin, see my tip on page 52. Serve while hot, and enjoy.

SMOKED CHICKEN BREASTS

Lots of folks will tell you that boneless, skinless chicken breasts are best grilled, but they won't have that wonderful smoky flavor—and since this is what we're after, I encourage you to use the smoker instead! When smoke cooked properly, chicken breasts will be tender, juicy, and delicious. After you try this recipe, I don't think you'll ever do them any other way. Instead of mixing your own dried spices, you can also use a store-bought seasoning made especially for chicken.

RECOMMENDED WOOD Apple
ESTIMATED COOK TIME 2½ hours
SERVES 6

6 boneless, skinless chicken breasts
   (about 3 lb)
1 tsp cayenne pepper
1 Tbsp table salt
1 tsp dried rosemary leaves
1 Tbsp garlic powder
1 lb thick-sliced fatty bacon, chopped
   in half

VARIATIONS

• Top the smoked chicken breasts with mango chutney or Pineapple Salsa (page 190), which is my favorite!
• Cut the smoked chicken into ½-inch cubes and serve over a garden salad.
• Make a chicken sandwich with lettuce, tomato, onion, mayonnaise, and barbecue sauce on whole wheat bread.

PREPARATION Brine the chicken breasts, if desired (see pages 37–40).

Rinse the chicken breasts under cold water and pat them dry with a paper towel. Mix together the cayenne, salt, rosemary, and garlic powder, and sprinkle about ½ Tbsp onto each breast. Set the chicken breasts aside for 30 to 45 minutes to absorb the flavor of the rub while you set up your smoker.

SMOKING Prepare your smoker for cooking at 225°F to 240°F. If you are using a gas, an electric, or a charcoal smoker, make sure you have enough wood chips or chunks on hand to produce smoke for about one hour.

Once the smoker is ready, place the breasts on the grate with about 1 inch of space between each one. To keep the meat moist while it smokes, cover the top of each breast with about three half-pieces of the bacon. The bacon will render and baste the chicken as it cooks.

Insert a digital probe meat thermometer into one of the breasts about one hour into the cooking session. Remove the chicken from the smoker as soon as it reaches 165°F, about two and a half hours in total. Serve immediately or keep the chicken breasts warm in a pan with foil tented over the top.

SMOKED CHICKEN THIGHS/LEGS

In my opinion, the most delicious part of a chicken is the dark meat; thighs and legs rule when it comes to flavor. I like to smoke these in large quantities; they are excellent snacks, reheat well in the microwave, and make me happy.

RECOMMENDED WOOD Pecan and
  apple at a 50:50 ratio
ESTIMATED COOK TIME 3 hours
SERVES 5 to 6

---

24 oz bottle Italian dressing
  (zesty is best if you can find it)
¼ cup orange juice
2 Tbsp garlic powder
2 Tbsp coarsely ground black pepper
1 Tbsp kosher salt
1 tsp cayenne pepper
1 tsp red pepper flakes
10 to 12 chicken bone-in thighs
  and/or legs, skin on

PREPARATION To make the marinade, combine the Italian dressing, orange juice, garlic powder, pepper, salt, cayenne, and red pepper flakes in a large Ziploc bag. Place the chicken pieces in the bag and seal the top. Roll the bag end over end to coat the chicken pieces with the liquid, then set it in the refrigerator overnight (or for at least four hours) to marinate. If you need to split the chicken into two or more bags, simply mix the marinade in a bowl and pour equal amounts into each bag with the chicken.

Remove the chicken from the refrigerator about 30 to 45 minutes before placing it in the smoker to bring it up to room temperature.

SMOKING Prepare the smoker for cooking at 225°F to 240°F. If you are using a gas, an electric, or a charcoal smoker, be sure to have enough wood chips or chunks to produce smoke for at least two hours.

Once the smoker is ready, place the chicken pieces directly on the grate, leaving about 1 inch between the pieces to allow maximum exposure to the smoke.

At about the two-hour mark, insert a digital probe meat thermometer into the thickest part of one of the thighs. Smoke cook the chicken for three to four hours in total, or until the internal temperature registers 165°F. Let the meat rest about 10 minutes before serving. If you want to crispen the skin, see my tip on page 52.

SMOKED WHOLE TURKEY

Most of us eat turkey only once or twice a year—at Thanksgiving and possibly at Christmas. However, once you taste smoked turkey prepared in your own smoker, you may find yourself wanting it a little more often.

RECOMMENDED WOOD Plum, apple,
   or mesquite
ESTIMATED COOK TIME 6½ hours
SERVES 10 to 12

1 whole turkey (about 12 lb)
½ cup All-Purpose Rub (page 146)

PREPARATION Rinse the turkey inside and out in cold water and pat dry with a paper towel. If you are going to brine the turkey, do that now by following the instructions on pages 37–40. You may decide to inject the bird instead by following the instructions on page 37.

After brining or injecting and/or before smoking, apply the All-Purpose Rub on the outside of the turkey and under the skin if possible. Leave the turkey sitting on the counter to bring it up to room temperature while you set up your smoker.

SMOKING Prepare your smoker for cooking at 225°F to 240°F. If you are using a gas, an electric, or a charcoal smoker, make sure to have enough smoking wood to last about three to four hours.

Place the turkey breast side down directly on the smoker grate. After one hour, flip the turkey breast side up to protect this tender meat from the direct heat. At this time, it is also a good idea to insert a digital probe meat thermometer into the thickest part of the breast or thigh to prevent a later loss of juices. If the wings, breast, or other parts of the turkey start to get too brown, cover them with small pieces of foil.

Smoke the turkey for another five and a half hours or until the thermometer reads 165°F. Remove the turkey from the smoker and allow it to rest for 30 minutes before carving. If you want to crispen the skin, see my tip on page 52.

SMOKED FRIED TURKEY

In the southern United States—and, I'm sure, in other areas—turkeys are deep-fried and delicious. I really like a smoked turkey as well, so this recipe attempts to achieve a turkey nirvana of sorts. The method may not be for everyone, since it requires a turkey fryer, but if you have one or know of someone who will lend you one, it is well worth your time to try this out.

RECOMMENDED WOOD Mesquite or hickory

ESTIMATED COOK TIME 2 hours

SERVES 10 to 12

1 whole turkey (about 12 lb)

3 to 5 gallons peanut oil (or other deep-frying oil)

PREPARATION Before you remove the bird from its package, drop it into your empty turkey fryer so you can determine how much oil you will need for the deep-frying step. Simply pour cold water into the fryer until the bird is covered, then remove the turkey and measure the amount of water you have used.

Rinse the turkey inside and out with cold water and pat dry with a paper towel. Brine the bird if desired (see page 37).

Set the turkey aside to bring it up to room temperature while you set up your smoker.

SMOKING Prepare your smoker for cooking at 225°F to 240°F. If you are using a gas, an electric, or a charcoal smoker, be sure to have enough wood chips or chunks on hand to produce about one and a half hours of smoke.

Once the smoker is ready, place the turkey directly on the grate breast side up and smoke cook it for one and a half hours.

While the bird is smoking, set up the turkey fryer by following the manufacturer's directions. IMPORTANT: Follow the instructions carefully—turkey fryers are extremely dangerous and many fires and injuries are caused every year.

Once the oil has been added and the turkey fryer is ready, and the turkey has smoke cooked for one and a half hours, lower the turkey very slowly and carefully into the hot oil (normally heated to 375°F), and deep-fry it for about two to two and a half minutes per pound. A 12-pound bird should take about 30 minutes to reach 165°F (be sure to use a thermometer to verify that the turkey has reached this temperature).

Remove the turkey from the fryer and let it rest for about 20 minutes before carving.

SMOKED TURKEY BREAST

Smoked turkey breast is my personal favorite, and this is very strange considering I never used to like turkey much, let alone the white meat. Several years ago, though, I started experimenting with brining, and it has changed my entire attitude about this bird. I now enjoy turkey, and what's more, I prefer the breast over any other part.

RECOMMENDED WOOD Pecan and
   cherry at a 50:50 ratio

ESTIMATED COOK TIME 4 to 6 hours

SERVES 6

---

1 bone-in turkey breast, skin on
   (about 5 to 7 lb)

2 Tbsp kosher salt

2 Tbsp coarsely ground black pepper

1 medium onion, quartered

1 cup apple juice or Apple Butter
   Mop (page 156)

PREPARATION Rinse the turkey breast under cold water and pat dry with a paper towel. If you want to brine the turkey overnight (which I highly recommend), follow the instructions on page 37. The brining process produces a much juicier and more flavorful turkey breast.

After brining and/or before smoking, sprinkle the turkey breast with the salt and pepper. Place the quartered onion into the cavity of the turkey breast. Set the meat aside on the counter for about 30 to 45 minutes to come up to room temperature while you set up your smoker.

Note: If you choose to use skinless turkey, you will need to replace the protection that the skin provides so the meat does not dry out in the smoker. To do this, wrap the entire breast in cheesecloth, then rub 1 cup (2 sticks) of cold butter onto the cloth to help keep the turkey moist during the first part of the cooking session. Sprinkle on some additional salt and pepper for good measure.

SMOKING Prepare your smoker for cooking at 225°F to 240°F. If you are using a gas, an electric, or a charcoal smoker, be sure to have enough wood chips or chunks on hand to produce smoke for at least three hours.

Place the turkey breast directly on the smoker grate and insert a digital probe meat thermometer into the thickest part of the meat. Baste the turkey every 45 minutes with the apple juice or Apple Butter Mop to keep the meat moist and tasty.

Smoke the turkey breast for four to six hours or until it reaches 165°F. Remove it from the smoker and set it on the counter tented with foil to rest for 20 minutes prior to carving. If you want to crispen the skin, see my tip on page 52.

SMOKED TURKEY LEGS

I have fond memories of going to the fair as a youngster and eating deliciously smoked turkey legs wrapped in foil. They were steaming hot when you opened the foil. The taste, as I remember it, was pretty unbelievable. My version of this special treat is about as good as it gets.

RECOMMENDED WOOD Pecan and mesquite at a 50:50 ratio

ESTIMATED COOK TIME 4 hours

SERVES 6

6 large turkey legs

1 gallon Jeff's Turkey Leg Brine (page 155), or enough to cover the meat

½ cup (1 stick) butter, melted

½ cup maple syrup

PREPARATION Rinse the turkey legs in cold water and place them in Jeff's Turkey Leg Brine for three to four hours. Once they are finished brining, rinse them again in cold water and pat dry with a paper towel. Let the turkey legs sit on the counter for 30 to 45 minutes to bring them up to room temperature while you set up your smoker.

SMOKING Prepare your smoker for cooking at 225°F to 240°F. If you are using a charcoal, an electric, or a gas smoker, make sure you have enough wood chips or chunks to produce about two hours of smoke.

Once the smoker is ready, place the turkey legs on the grate, leaving about 1 inch between the pieces for maximum exposure to the smoke. Insert a digital probe meat thermometer into the thickest part of one of the turkey legs so you can monitor the temperature of the meat as it cooks.

Combine the butter and maple syrup, and use this to baste the legs every 45 minutes, making sure to get the mixture on all sides. A silicone brush will help with this process.

Once the legs reach 140°F, increase the heat of the smoker to around 275°F to crispen the skin and caramelize the maple syrup.

Continue smoking the legs until they reach an internal temperature of 165°F, about four hours in total. Remove them from the smoker and allow them to rest for about 20 minutes before eating. For a true fair-like experience, wrap them in foil as soon as they come off the smoker.

SMOKED DUCK WITH WINE BUTTER SAUCE

Duck may not be everyone's cup of tea, but I implore you to try it smoked and you might just change your mind about this feathered friend. A few hours with some nice sweet smoke does something magical to duck, and I find myself picking the carcass clean every single time. This particular version with wine sauce comes to us from CycleTrash at www.smokingmeatforums.com.

RECOMMENDED WOOD Apple and
  cherry at a 50:50 ratio
ESTIMATED COOK TIME 4 hours
SERVES 6

3 whole ducks
1½ gallons buttermilk
½ cup All-Purpose Rub (page 146)
3 apples
3 onions, quartered
1 recipe Wine Butter Sauce (below)

PREPARATION Soak the ducks in the buttermilk overnight (12 to 24 hours) to remove any gamey taste in the meat.

Rinse the ducks in cold water and pat dry with a paper towel. Season inside and out with the All-Purpose Rub. Place a whole unpeeled apple and a quartered onion inside the cavity of each duck. Let the ducks sit to bring them up to room temperature, while you set up your smoker.

SMOKING Prepare your smoker for cooking at 225°F to 240°F. If you are using a charcoal, an electric, or a gas smoker, be sure to have enough wood chips or chunks to produce smoke for at least two hours.

Once the smoker is ready, place the ducks breast side up on the smoker grate. Insert a digital probe meat thermometer in the thickest part of one breast to monitor the internal temperature of the meat. Baste the ducks every hour with the Wine Butter Sauce.

Smoke cook the ducks for about four hours or until the internal temperature reaches 165°F. To crispen the skin, follow the instructions on page 52.

WINE BUTTER SAUCE

MAKES about 1¼ cups

1 cup (2 sticks) butter
1½ cups red wine (not cooking wine)
2 Tbsp minced garlic

This recipe works best with smoked duck (above), but it also complements other poultry.

Place all ingredients in a medium saucepan set over medium heat. Mix well and simmer until the sauce reduces by half.

SMOKED HOT WINGS

*Is there anything better than hot wings? My wife, Abi, always cooks my
favorite meal on my birthday, and I always ask for hot wings. She does
a fantastic job, but what makes these delicious morsels of goodness even
better is to add a little smoked flavor to the mix. This recipe will show you
how that's done. (In case you were wondering, I do the smoking and
she still does the coating and frying parts of the recipe.)*

RECOMMENDED WOOD Mesquite and
  hickory at a 50:50 ratio
ESTIMATED COOK TIME 2 hours
SERVES 6 to 8

4 lb chicken wings or drumettes
3 cups vegetable oil (approx)
1 cup (2 sticks) butter, melted
2 cups all-purpose flour
2 cups wing sauce (I like Frank's
  RedHot Original Cayenne Pepper
  Sauce, but other brands will work,
  or you can make your own using
  the recipes on the next page)

PREPARATION Rinse the chicken wings or drumettes in cold
water and pat dry with a paper towel. Set the chicken aside
for about 20 to 30 minutes to allow it to come up to room
temperature while you set up your smoker.

SMOKING Prepare your smoker for cooking at 225°F to 240°F.
If you are using a charcoal, an electric, or a gas smoker, be sure
to have enough wood chips or chunks to produce smoke for
about two hours.

 Place the chicken pieces on the grate and smoke cook for
about two hours, or until the chicken is close to being done
(about 150°F; the small size of these pieces of chicken makes it
difficult to measure the temperature, so insert a thermometer
as well as you can into the thickest part of a drumette). I don't
worry about cooking these wings completely in the smoker,
since the frying step cooks them further. However, if you
decide not to fry them, make sure that the chicken pieces are
165°F before removing them from the smoker.

FRYING In a large iron skillet, heat a ½ inch of the oil to 375°F.
Brush each piece of smoked chicken with the melted butter,
roll it in the flour, and place it into the hot oil. Fry the chicken
pieces for 45 seconds, then turn them over and fry for another
45 seconds. Lay the fried pieces on a paper towel to drain as
they come out of the pan. Repeat this process until all the
wings and drumettes are finished frying.

(CONTINUED NEXT PAGE)

SMOKED HOT WINGS (CONTINUED)

FINAL PREPARATION Brush each piece of fried chicken with the wing sauce—or if you want to do it right and don't mind a little mess, put a little of the sauce and some of the chicken pieces (I like to do a dozen at a time) together into a lidded plastic bowl or a large Ziploc bag, and toss to coat. Repeat until you have coated all of the chicken with sauce.

Place the chicken pieces in a pan in a warm oven until all of the chicken is ready to serve.

BASIC WING SAUCE

ESTIMATED COOK TIME 20 minutes
MAKES about 1¾ cups

---

1 cup Frank's RedHot Original
   Cayenne Pepper Sauce
½ cup (1 stick) butter
¼ cup light brown sugar (optional)

Place the Frank's RedHot sauce and butter, and, if you want the wing sauce to be a tad sweet, the brown sugar, into a small pot on low heat. After the butter is completely melted, let the mixture simmer gently for 15 minutes.

HOT BARBECUE WING SAUCE

ESTIMATED COOK TIME 20 minutes
MAKES about 2 cups

---

1 cup thick tomato-based barbecue
   sauce
½ cup Louisiana Wildly Wicked Wing
   Sauce (or another brand of really
   hot wing sauce)
½ cup (1 stick) butter

Place all ingredients into a small pot on low heat. After the butter is completely melted, let the mixture simmer gently for 15 minutes.

MONSTER WINGS

This is something I came up with a few years back due to my intense love for hot wings. I use regular sized chicken legs instead of the smaller portions of wings or drumettes that you would normally use. To up the ante on the meat-to-sauce ratio, I inject the wing sauce into the meat and pour it over the outside just before serving. This is truly man-food, but the ladies will probably like them just as well.

RECOMMENDED WOOD Mesquite and hickory at a 50:50 ratio

ESTIMATED COOK TIME 2 hours

SERVES 6 to 8

4 lb chicken legs

3 cups vegetable oil (amount depends on the size of your pan)

1 cup (2 sticks) butter, melted

2 cups all-purpose flour

2 cups wing sauce (I like Frank's RedHot Original Cayenne Pepper Sauce, but other brands will work, or you can make your own using the recipes on the previous page)

PREPARATION Rinse the chicken legs in cool water and pat dry with a paper towel. Use a meat injector to inject about half an ounce of the wing sauce into the thickest part of each leg. Inject half of the sauce into one side, then rotate the leg 180 degrees and inject the other half of the sauce into the opposite side. Once you are finished injecting the sauce into the chicken legs, set them aside while you set up your smoker.

SMOKING Prepare your smoker for cooking at 225°F to 240°F. If you are using a charcoal, an electric, or a gas smoker, be sure to have enough wood chips or chunks to produce smoke for about two hours.

Place the chicken legs on the grate and smoke cook for about two hours, or until the chicken is 165°F using a meat thermometer in the thickest part of the leg.

FRYING (OPTIONAL) I enjoy the crispy texture that frying adds to the outside and I think you will too. Pour about three-quarters of an inch of oil into a large, iron skillet and heat to 375°F. Brush each smoked chicken leg with butter, roll it in flour, and place it into the hot oil. Fry the legs for about one minute, turn over, and fry for another minute to brown and crisp the outside. Repeat until all of the legs are fried. As you take each leg out of the pan, lay it on a paper towel to drain.

FINAL PREPARATION Brush each piece of fried chicken with wing sauce. Or put a few at a time into a large Ziploc bag with some sauce, zip up the bag, and toss to coat. Place the coated chicken legs in a pan in a warm oven until ready to serve.

SMOKED CORNISH GAME HENS

*One of my earliest recollections of eating these little hens is when
I was visiting the Dixie Stampede in Branson, Missouri, where
they are served with piles of side dishes, not to mention bread
and iced sweet tea—and no utensils are allowed.*

*I love to smoke these, and it is not uncommon at my house for these to
show up on the menu for special occasions with close friends and family.*

RECOMMENDED WOOD Mesquite and
   hickory at a 50:50 ratio
ESTIMATED COOK TIME 4 hours
SERVES 4

4 Cornish game hens
2 Tbsp All-Purpose Rub (page 146)
½ cup (1 stick) butter, melted

PREPARATION Rinse the hens with cold water and pat
dry with a paper towel. If you wish to brine them (which I
recommend), follow the instructions on pages 37–40, leaving
the hens in the brine for about two hours.

After brining and/or before smoking, sprinkle each hen
with approximately ½ Tbsp of the All-Purpose Rub, making
sure to get some of the seasoning under the skin wherever
possible.

Leave the hens on the counter for 30 to 45 minutes to come
up to room temperature while you set up your smoker.

SMOKING Prepare your smoker for cooking at 225°F to 240°F.
If you are using a charcoal, an electric, or a gas smoker, be
sure to have enough wood chips or chunks on hand to produce
smoke for at least two hours.

Once the smoker is ready, place the hens directly on the
grate breast side up. Baste the hens with the melted butter
every 45 minutes throughout the cooking process.

Smoke the hens for about four hours or until a digital probe
meat thermometer inserted in the thickest part of the breast
or thigh reads 165°F. (The thermometer can be inserted at the
beginning of the cook time, or you can wait until the hens have
been in the smoker for about two hours.)

Place the hens in a pan tented with foil and let them rest
for 15 minutes before serving. If you want to crispen the skin,
follow the instructions on page 52.

SMOKED CHICKEN GUMBO WITH ANDOUILLE

Amp up traditional Cajun gumbo by using smoked chicken. The roux is the most important component of this dish, so make sure you have time to spend in the kitchen, stirring leisurely without interruption. It's fascinating to watch the flour and oil slowly brown to a dark chocolate color, layer by layer. As when smoking meat, patience is the key.

ESTIMATED COOK TIME 2 hours

SERVES 10

1½ cups all-purpose flour

1 cup + 2 Tbsp vegetable oil

2 small onions, diced

2 green bell peppers, diced

4 stalks celery, chopped

1 whole chicken (about 4 lb), smoked (page 55), cooled, deboned, and pulled into pieces

1 lb andouille or smoked sausage, thinly sliced

8 cups chicken broth

1 Tbsp Cajun seasoning (such as Tony Chachere's Original Creole Seasoning), or to taste

1 tsp Tabasco sauce, or to taste

1 bunch green onions, green parts only, thinly sliced

ROUX In a heavy pan (I use a cast iron pan), whisk together the flour and 1 cup of the oil. Heat carefully over low heat, whisking for a smooth consistency and using a spatula to keep the roux from sticking to the bottom of the pan. Slowly cook the roux until it turns the color of dark chocolate and smells toasted; this takes about one hour for a typical batch. Do not burn or scorch the roux, or you'll have to start over. Remove the roux from the heat and set aside to cool. IMPORTANT: Do not taste the roux during or directly after cooking. It is very hot and will burn your mouth or skin.

After the roux has cooled, pour off any oil that has separated, and use only the thicker roux that is left behind. This reduces the amount of fat in this dish.

GUMBO In a frying pan, heat the remaining 2 Tbsp of oil over medium heat. Sauté the onions, bell peppers, and celery until just tender, about 10 to 12 minutes. Remove the vegetables from the heat and place them in a stockpot. Add the deboned chicken, sliced sausage, and chicken broth. Bring to a rolling boil over medium-high heat.

To add the cooled roux to the pot, spoon a couple of tablespoons into a heavy bowl and whisk in 1 cup of the hot chicken broth. Once the mixture is smooth, add more roux and a bit more chicken broth, and whisk again. Continue until you've used all the roux, then whisk the mixture back into the pot with the rest of the broth, vegetables, and meat. Add the Cajun seasoning and Tabasco, adjusting the amounts to taste.

Reduce the heat to low, cover, and simmer for 20 to 30 minutes, stirring occasionally. Serve over rice or with Abi's Classic Potato Salad (page 182). Top with the green onions.

TIPS FOR SMOKING PORK

GETTING IT TENDER

Most of the pork that we commonly smoke is safe to eat at 160°F; however, this is usually not the temperature at which the meat is best to eat. Cuts such as ribs and pork shoulder should be left in the smoker until they are tender, regardless of what their internal temperature might be. When cooking ribs, I don't even check the temperature of the meat; ribs are still chewy at 160°F and should be left to idle in the smoker until they pass a tenderness test (see page 15). Pork butt is not at its best until it reaches 185°F to 190°F, and if you want to pull it I recommend letting it go to 205°F, when it will be juicy and will fall apart with very little work.

On the other hand, pork cuts that are not commonly smoked, such as tenderloin or chops, do not get more tender the longer they stay in the smoker. They should be cooked just until safe to eat, which is 160°F as recommended by the United States Department of Agriculture and the Canadian Food Inspection Agency.

WHAT'S IN A NAME?

I have used what I consider the most common terminology to describe pork cuts in this book, but it may be helpful for you to know the following: *Baby back ribs* are also called *loin back ribs*. *Pork butt* is also called *Boston butt*. *Pork steaks* are also called *pork blade steaks*.

2

PORK

SHOULDERS, BUTTS, AND PICNICS

Pork shoulder is usually cut into two pieces, the butt and the picnic. The butt has a bone, whereas the picnic is boneless. I prefer the butt for making pulled pork because the meat is of a higher quality and it does not have a thick skin on one side like the picnic does. Pork butt is sometimes cut into pork steaks or into long, rib-like pieces called country-style ribs.

REMOVING THE MEMBRANE AND FLAP OF MEAT ON RIBS

The membrane is a thick piece of plastic-like skin found on pork baby back and spare ribs, as well as on beef back ribs. If not removed, it will prevent smoke and flavorings from penetrating the meat, which will greatly diminish the eating experience. You can easily remove the membrane by inserting a knife or other sharp object under one corner and prying it up. Then, use a paper towel to grip the membrane and pull it completely off. If it tears, just pry it up again and repeat the same process until all of the membrane is removed.

Spare ribs have a flap of meat running along the length of the ribs; this should be removed before smoking. To do so, pull up on the flap and cut it with a sharp knife held downward at a 45-degree angle. Do not discard this piece of meat, as it makes a great snack. Just add a little rub to it and place it on the grate along with your ribs. It will be ready to eat in about two hours. Chef's treat!

SMOKED PORK SPARE RIBS

Spare ribs come from the belly of the pig, and being fattier than the baby backs, they take longer to cook and require more patience to get them tender. But if you give them time and lots of tender loving care, you might just decide they are well worth it. The payback in flavor is amazing, and when smoked up right, these are fit for a king!

RECOMMENDED WOOD Apple, cherry, or hickory

ESTIMATED COOK TIME 6 hours

SERVES 6

---

2 racks pork spare ribs (about 4 lb or more per rack)

¼ cup yellow mustard

⅓ cup Big Bald BBQ Rub (page 148)

1 cup apple juice (or other fruit juice)

PREPARATION Rinse the spare ribs with cold water and pat dry with a paper towel. Place them on a cutting board bone side up, and remove the flap of meat running along the length of the ribs as well as the membrane (see previous page).

Once the ribs are trimmed, apply a light coating of the mustard on both sides, then sprinkle the rub on both sides. Leave the ribs on the counter for 20 to 30 minutes to come up to room temperature while you set up your smoker.

SMOKING Prepare your smoker for cooking at 225°F to 240°F. If you are using a charcoal, a gas, or an electric smoker, make sure to have enough wood chips or chunks to produce about three to four hours of smoke.

Place the spare ribs flat on the grate, bone side down. After the ribs have been in the smoker for two hours, begin spritzing them with the apple juice once every hour. A plastic spray bottle works great for this purpose.

Spare ribs are done when they are tender (see page 15), which should take around six hours. Transfer the cooked racks to a cutting board and slice into individual ribs. Serve immediately. These go really well with Dutch's Wicked Baked Beans (see page 179).

SMOKED BABY BACKS

While some might say that spare ribs are king, baby backs are really hard to beat when it comes to the meat:fat ratio. Baby backs are taken from the loin of the pig, where there is less fat and the meat is naturally more tender. This means that baby backs usually cook faster and become tender at a lower internal temperature.

RECOMMENDED WOOD Apple, cherry, or hickory

ESTIMATED COOK TIME 5 hours

SERVES 4

---

2 racks baby back pork ribs (about 2 lb per rack)

¼ cup yellow mustard

¼ cup Big Bald BBQ Rub (page 148)

1 cup apple juice (or other fruit juice)

PREPARATION Rinse the ribs with cold water and pat dry with a paper towel. Place them on a cutting board bone side up and remove the membrane (see page 78).

Once the ribs are trimmed, apply a light coat of the yellow mustard to both sides, then sprinkle the rub on both sides, making sure to coat the edges as well. Leave the ribs on the counter for 20 to 30 minutes to come up to room temperature while you set up your smoker.

SMOKING Prepare your smoker for cooking at 225°F to 240°F. If you are using a charcoal, a gas, or an electric smoker, make sure to have enough wood chips or chunks to produce three to four hours of smoke.

Lay the ribs flat on the grate for best results; the melted fat will pool on top of the ribs and keep them moist. If space is a problem, the ribs can also be cut in half, placed vertically on a rib rack, or rolled into a barrel and held together with a long skewer.

After the ribs have been in the smoker for two hours, begin spritzing them with the apple juice once every hour. A plastic spray bottle works great for this purpose.

The ribs are done when they are tender (see page 15), which should require about five hours of smoking.

Once the ribs are removed from the smoker, allow them to rest for 15 to 20 minutes before slicing. Ribs are easiest to slice when you place them bone side up on a cutting board so you can see the bones.

SMOKED PORK BUTT

*Although pork butt is one of the most time-consuming pieces of meat
you will ever cook on the smoker, it is also one of the easiest and most
forgiving. My favorite way to eat smoked pork butt is to pull it and pile it
high on a bun with lots of barbecue sauce and coleslaw (see page 184).
It is also delicious when used in tacos, in burritos, on a pizza, in shepherd's
pie, or atop a salad—the options are limited only by your imagination.*

RECOMMENDED WOOD Pecan and
apple at a 50:50 ratio

ESTIMATED COOK TIME 10½ to
12 hours (1½ hours per pound)

SERVES 6 to 8

---

7 to 8 lb pork butt

¼ cup yellow mustard

1 cup Big Bald BBQ Rub (page 148)

PREPARATION Rinse the pork butt under cold water and pat
dry with a paper towel. Apply a light coat of the mustard to the
entire exterior of the meat, making sure to get the mustard
down into any folds and crevices.

Pour the rub onto the top of the pork butt, and use your
hands to massage it into the meat. As the rub mixes with the
mustard it creates a great-tasting paste that will stay on the
meat during the cooking process.

Leave the pork butt on the counter for 30 to 45 minutes to
come up to room temperature while you set up your smoker.

SMOKING Prepare your smoker for cooking at 225°F to 240°F.
If you are using a gas, an electric, or a charcoal smoker, be
sure to have enough wood chips or chunks on hand to produce
smoke for about five to six hours.

Once the smoker is ready, place the pork butt directly on the
grate. Place a pan under the grate to catch the drippings as the
meat cooks. (You could also cook the pork butt in a disposable
aluminum pan.)

At about the four-hour mark, insert a digital probe meat
thermometer into the thickest part of the meat. Smoke cook
until the thermometer reads 205°F (this should take about
one and a half hours per pound). Remove the meat from the
smoker and allow it to rest for 30 minutes before pulling it.

Transfer the drippings you have collected into a lidded
container and place it in the refrigerator to cool.

(CONTINUED ON PAGE 84)

SMOKED PORK BUTT (CONTINUED)

PULLING Remove the bone from the pork butt by sliding it out (this should be very easy if the pork is cooked to 205°F). Use two forks to pull the meat apart into small chunks.

Remove the cold pork drippings from the refrigerator, and skim off and discard the fat that has solidified at the top. What remains is the tasty *jus*, which can be mixed in with the pulled pork to add lots of flavor to the meat.

3-2-1 RIBS

*At barbecue competitions, ribs are supposed to be just tender enough,
not too tender. However, I often hear people speak longingly about
the ribs they once ate that were so tender the meat just
"fell right off the bone." The method below is a very good
way to achieve these folks' rib nirvana.*

RECOMMENDED WOOD Hickory and
pecan at a 50:50 ratio

ESTIMATED COOK TIME 6 hours

SERVES 6

---

2 racks pork spare ribs (about 4 lb
or more per rack)

¼ cup yellow mustard

⅓ cup Big Bald BBQ Rub (page 148)

½ cup apple juice

PREPARATION Rinse the spare ribs with cold water and pat dry with a paper towel. Place them on a cutting board bone side up, and remove the flap of meat running along the length of the ribs, as well as the membrane (see page 78).

Once the ribs are trimmed, apply a thin coat of the mustard on both sides, then sprinkle the rub evenly on both sides of the meat. Let the ribs sit for 20 to 30 minutes to come up to room temperature while you set up your smoker.

SMOKING Prepare your smoker for cooking at 225°F to 240°F. If you are using a gas, an electric, or a charcoal smoker, be sure to have enough wood chips or chunks to produce smoke for about three hours.

Place the ribs flat on the grate, bone side down. You can also use a holder or rack to hold multiple racks of ribs in a vertical position if your smoker is limited on space.

Allow the spare ribs to smoke cook for three hours at 225°F to 240°F, then remove them from the smoker grate and lay each on a piece of high-quality heavy-duty foil cut big enough to enclose each rack completely. Pour about ¼ cup of the apple juice onto each rack and quickly close the foil around the ribs. Place the foil-wrapped ribs back on the smoker grate and cook for two more hours.

Remove the ribs from the smoker grate, take them out of the foil, and place them back on the smoker grate for one more hour. This final hour firms up the ribs a bit and helps them regain some crispiness on the outside, while still leaving them very tender inside. Transfer the cooked racks to a cutting board and slice into individual ribs. Serve immediately.

AL'S 3-2-1 ASIAN RIBS

Al, known as FMCowboy at www.smokingmeatforums.com,
sent me this recipe, and once I tried it I knew it had to be shared.
The Asian accent in this recipe really comes out and takes the ribs
to a brand new level. These ribs are smoked using the 3-2-1 method,
for that super-tender effect that many people love.

RECOMMENDED WOOD Pecan and mesquite at a 50:50 ratio
ESTIMATED COOK TIME 6 hours
SERVES 6

2 racks pork spare ribs (about 4 lb or more per rack)
3 Tbsp low-sodium soy sauce
⅓ cup Asian Rub (page 151)
1 cup apple juice
1 cup Asian Sauce (page 146)

PREPARATION Rinse the spare ribs with cold water and pat dry with a paper towel. Place them on a cutting board bone side up, and remove the flap of meat running along the length of the ribs, as well as the membrane (see page 78).

Once the ribs are trimmed, apply a light coating of the soy sauce to both sides, then sprinkle the Asian Rub evenly on both sides. Let the ribs sit on the counter while you set up your smoker.

SMOKING Prepare your smoker for cooking at 225°F to 240°F. If you are using a gas, an electric, or a charcoal smoker, be sure to have enough wood chips or chunks on hand to produce smoke for at least three hours.

Place the ribs flat on the grate, bone side down. Smoke cook them for three hours, spritzing with the apple juice after the second hour. A plastic spray bottle works well for this purpose.

After three hours, remove the ribs quickly and place each rack on a piece of high-quality heavy-duty foil. Spritz the ribs with apple juice, wrap them completely in foil, and place them back on the grate for two hours.

Once two hours have elapsed, take the ribs off the smoker grate and remove the foil. Place the ribs back on the grate, bone side down, for an additional hour to firm them back up and finish cooking them. During this last hour of cooking, brush both sides of the ribs with the Asian Sauce every 30 minutes until they reach the tenderness that you desire.

When the ribs are done, remove them from the smoker grate and let them rest about 10 to 15 minutes before slicing. Serve hot, over rice and chopped green onions, with warm Asian Sauce on the side.

BRUNSWICK STEW WITH SMOKED PORK

*If you like Brunswick stew as much as I do, you'll find yourself making
this dish time and time again. It tastes even better the second day—
if there's any left over, that is! This recipe is a modified version
of the one sent to me by my friend Gene Smith, who says it makes
a wonderful camp food when deer hunting. You can also use
smoked chicken instead of the pulled Smoked Pork Butt.*

ESTIMATED COOK TIME 45 minutes

SERVES 6 to 8

⅓ cup vegetable oil (bacon fat is even
    better if you have it)
1 medium onion, chopped
3 stalks celery, trimmed and chopped
1 green bell pepper, diced
6 cups pulled Smoked Pork Butt
    (page 82)
28 oz can diced tomatoes
28 oz can tomato sauce
28 oz can creamed corn
3 large russet potatoes, peeled
    and cubed
1 cup beer (or water)
¼ cup barbecue sauce (try Slim's
    Sweet & Sticky Barbecue Sauce
    page 140)
1 Tbsp + 1 tsp table salt
1 tsp chili powder
½ tsp coarsely ground black pepper
¼ tsp cayenne pepper (or 1 tsp
    Tabasco sauce)

Heat the oil or bacon fat in a large frying pan over medium
heat. Sauté the onion, celery, and bell pepper until tender,
about 10 minutes.

Transfer the vegetables to a large stockpot and add the
remaining ingredients. Bring to a boil over medium heat,
stirring often to prevent sticking. Reduce the heat and simmer
for 30 minutes, or until the potatoes are easily pierced with
a fork.

Serve with cornbread.

SMOKING GUN'S PULLED PORK SHEPHERD'S PIE

Smoking Gun, a member at www.smokingmeatforums.com, wanted a way to use up leftover pulled pork, so he cooked up some mashed potatoes and came up with this wonderful southern version of shepherd's pie. His family loved it and the rest is history. I love it too, and so will you!

ESTIMATED COOK TIME 20 minutes

SERVES 6 to 8

8 cups Garlic Mashed Potatoes
(page 172)
4 cups pulled Smoked Pork Butt
(page 82)
2 cups shredded pepper Jack cheese
4 cups shredded cheddar cheese

NOTE If you want to make individual portions in small casserole dishes or ramekins, divide each layer evenly by the number of individual dishes you are using.

Add the following layers to a deep casserole dish or lasagna pan in this order: 4 cups mashed potatoes; 4 cups pulled pork; 2 cups pepper Jack cheese; 2 cups cheddar cheese; 4 cups mashed potatoes; 2 cups cheddar cheese.

Once layered, bake the shepherd's pie in the oven, uncovered, at 350°F for 15 minutes.

PULLED PORK BREAKFAST BURRITOS

*Here's another great way to use up leftover smoked pulled pork,
brisket, or chicken. Who would have thought you could have
barbecue for breakfast? Well, now you can—and a mighty tasty
bit at that. Serve these with your favorite salsa and you might
just decide that morning is not so bad after all.*

ESTIMATED COOK TIME 20 minutes

SERVES 6

2 Tbsp vegetable or canola oil

1 red onion, julienned

1 green bell pepper, julienned

2 large jalapeño peppers, seeded and
   thinly sliced

2 cups pulled Smoked Pork Butt
   (page 82)

8 eggs, beaten

Six 12-inch flour tortillas

1 cup shredded pepper Jack cheese

½ cup sour cream (approx)

½ cup salsa (approx) (or Perfect Pico
   de Gallo [approx, page 189])

Heat the oil in a large frying pan set over medium-high heat.
Add the onion, bell pepper, and jalapeños, and sauté until
softened and lightly browned. Add the pulled pork and sauté
for one to two minutes longer, or until the pork is heated
through.

In a nonstick pan, scramble the eggs until set but soft.
Remove promptly and set aside.

On a tortilla, layer one-sixth of each of the pulled pork and
vegetables, scrambled eggs, and shredded cheese. Top with
the sour cream and salsa or pico de gallo, and wrap the tortilla
burrito-style. Repeat with the remaining tortillas. Serve
immediately.

BACON-WRAPPED STUFFED SAUSAGE FATTY

*What do you get when you roll out a breakfast sausage, stuff it full
of cheese and other goodies, roll it back up, wrap it with a weave of bacon,
then smoke it so it is nice and crispy on the outside and oozing with moist
goodness on the inside? Well, one of the best darn things you'll ever eat in
your whole life, that's what! I highly recommend making two of these,
as the first one will go so quick you won't even know what happened to it.*

RECOMMENDED WOOD Hickory,
  cherry, or pecan

ESTIMATED COOK TIME 3 hours

SERVES 6

---

13 strips thinly sliced bacon

1 lb plain or hot ground breakfast
  sausage

½ cup shredded pepper Jack cheese

1 jalapeño pepper, finely chopped

½ cup shredded cheddar cheese

8 to 10 baby spinach leaves

---

*See page 97 for photos of steps in
bacon weave and preparation.*

BACON WEAVE This isn't difficult, but it may take a little
practice to figure out exactly how to make it work.

Lay seven strips of the bacon in a horizontal fashion on an
18- × 18-inch piece of waxed paper. Remove strips two, four,
and six. Lay a single strip of bacon along the edge, across rows
one, three, five, and seven. This is column one.

Replace rows two, four, and six on top of column one.

Next, fold back rows one, three, five, and seven, and lay a
second column of bacon (column two) right beside column one
and across rows two, four, and six.

Replace rows one, three, five, and seven across column two.

Continue this pattern of weaving until you have completed a
seven- by six-piece bacon weave.

PREPARATION Place the sausage into a 1-gallon Ziploc bag.
Zip the top of the bag, then snip a bit off of the two bottom
corners to let air escape. Using a rolling pin, flatten the
sausage evenly so you have a perfectly formed square. Use a
sharp knife or scissors to cut the bag open along the seams.
Remove the top layer of the bag, leaving the sausage square on
the bottom.

Flip the sausage square onto an 18- × 18-inch piece of waxed
paper. Remove the plastic. Layer the top of the sausage with the
pepper Jack, jalapeño, cheddar, and spinach leaves.

Roll the sausage up, with the filling inside, using the
waxed paper to help you. Once the sausage is completely rolled
up, place the roll along the bottom row of the bacon weave,
centering it. Use the waxed paper that the bacon weave is lying

(CONTINUED NEXT PAGE)

BACON-WRAPPED STUFFED SAUSAGE FATTY (CONTINUED)

on to help you roll the bacon around the stuffed sausage roll.

Leave the fatty on the counter while you set up your smoker.

SMOKING Prepare your smoker for cooking at 225°F to 240°F. If you are using a gas, an electric, or a charcoal smoker, be sure to have enough wood chips or chunks to produce smoke for about two hours. Once the smoker is ready, carefully place the fatty directly on the smoker grate with the seam of the bacon weave facing down.

Smoke the fatty for three hours. Once it is done cooking, remove it from the smoker grate and let it rest for 15 minutes before slicing it into ½-inch medallions.

Eat the fatty slices for breakfast with eggs or on a burger or sandwich. Fatties even taste great on a plain piece of bread with a little barbecue sauce drizzled over the top.

SMOKED BRATWURST OR BOUDIN SAUSAGES

I lived in Louisiana for five years, and while I was there I developed a real love for Cajun food. Boudin was one of the items I thoroughly enjoyed, along with crawfish, tasso, and a whole slew of other foods I dare not get into. Boudin is wonderful smoked, and the method for smoking it is so similar to smoking brats that I have placed them together here, pointing out only a couple of differences. Boudin is basically rice with pork and spices made in a very tasty Cajun way; if you have not tried it, you are truly missing out. Brats are usually made from pork and veal, and are of German heritage.

RECOMMENDED WOOD Pecan, oak, or cherry

ESTIMATED COOK TIME 2 hours (bratwurst); 3 hours (boudin)

SERVES 5 to 6

10 to 12 bratwurst or boudin sausages

¼ cup barbecue sauce (optional)

PREPARATION Remove the sausages from their packaging and leave them on the counter while you set up your smoker.

SMOKING Prepare your smoker for cooking at 225°F to 240°F. If you are using a gas, an electric, or a charcoal smoker, be sure to have enough wood chips or chunks to produce smoke for about two hours.

Once the smoker is ready, place the sausages directly on the grate, leaving about 1 inch between them to allow full exposure to the smoke. Smoke brats for two hours (do not overcook), and boudin sausages for three hours. For added flavor on the brats, brush your favorite barbecue sauce onto the sausages about 15 minutes before they are finished smoking. Remove the cooked sausages from the grate and immediately place them in a pan covered with foil to keep them warm until serving.

TIPS FOR SMOKING BEEF

GRADES OF BEEF

The grading of beef has to do with the amount of intramuscular fat marbling in the meat. As you may know, this fat is very important when smoking meat at a low temperature for a long time. Fat marbling is directly related to flavor and tenderness, and while this may not be as important when smoking brisket, it is extremely important with cuts like prime rib.

In the United States, the top grade is *prime*, which is simply the best—and, of course, the most expensive. The next grade down is *choice*, followed by *select*. Select grade is likely what you are buying at your local grocery store, and it is okay for most purposes. I recommend buying the best you can afford.

3

BEEF

CHOOSING A GOOD BRISKET

Brisket is naturally tough, requiring many hours of cooking at low heat to become tender. It makes sense to me that the tenderer the brisket when you start, the better it will be when it is finished. For this reason, I recommend taking a few precautions when choosing the brisket you will take home with you.

First and foremost, if you are fortunate enough to find briskets wrapped in plastic alone, you can lay them, one at a time, across the side of your hand to see which has the most bend. The most flexible brisket is going to be the tenderest. Some briskets are sold on Styrofoam trays, which prevent the bend test from being performed.

It is also important to choose a brisket that has not been trimmed and still has a considerable fat cap on the top. The fat cap will render during the cooking session, naturally basting the top of the brisket. Look for a brisket marked as a "packer," which means that it is the complete untrimmed cut.

GROUND BEEF VS. GROUND CHUCK

In the smoked meatloaf recipes in this section, you will see that some call for ground beef while others call for ground chuck. You may be wondering what the difference is, and if it really matters which one you buy. Basically, it's all about where the meat comes from on the cow and the amount of fat content there is.

Ground beef comes from less desirable parts of the animal, and can even be from trimmings (it must not contain more than 30% fat.) Ground chuck comes from the chuck roast, and is a more popular cut of beef. Typically, it is leaner than ground beef. That said, do not go by the cut to determine how lean the meat is. Rather, go by the written fat content on the package, which is usually labeled as 90/10, 85/15, 80/20, or 73/27. The first number in the ratio is the meat content, and the second number is the fat.

For me, fat equals flavor. It also helps hold the beef together while it cooks. I recommend 80/20 ground beef or ground chuck for meatloaf.

GARLIC & ONION BRISKET

*If you are a garlic and onion freak like me, you will certainly appreciate
this tasty rendition of smoked brisket. I used this method to make brisket
for years before I decided to try new recipes, but the old way is still my
favorite for smoking a brisket that is melt-in-your-mouth good.*

RECOMMENDED WOOD Mesquite

ESTIMATED COOK TIME 10½ to
13½ hours (1½ hours per pound)

SERVES 8

---

7 to 9 lb packer (untrimmed) brisket

1 recipe Garlic & Onion Paste (see
next page)

1 cup Jeff's Mop Water (page 157)

¼ cup barbecue sauce (optional)

PREPARATION Rinse the brisket and pat dry with a paper
towel. Place the brisket fat side up in a large pan or bowl, and
cover it completely with the Garlic and Onion Paste. Cover and
place in the refrigerator for 10 to 12 hours or overnight.

About one hour before smoking, take the brisket out of the
refrigerator and allow it to come up to room temperature.

SMOKING Prepare your smoker for a long cooking session
at 225°F to 240°F. If you are using a gas, an electric, or a
charcoal smoker, be sure to have enough wood chips or chunks
to produce smoke for about six hours.

Once the smoker is ready, remove the brisket from the
pan or bowl and place it directly on the smoker grate, fat side
up. After four hours of smoke cooking, begin mopping the
brisket every one and a half hours with the mop water. At every
mopping, flip the brisket to the opposite side (fat cap up, fat
cap down, etc.). Also at the four-hour mark, insert a digital
probe meat thermometer into the side of the brisket so that the
thermometer remains intact regardless of whether the meat is
fat side up or down. Anytime after about 10 hours, feel free to
brush on your favorite barbecue sauce to add some amazing
flavor to the crust.

Smoke cook the brisket for about one and a half hours per
pound, or until the meat reaches an internal temperature of
195°F. Once the brisket is finished cooking, remove it from the
smoker grate and allow it to rest for 30 minutes to allow the
juices to redistribute throughout the meat. Slice the brisket
across the grain into ¼- to ½-inch-thick pieces and serve with
warm barbecue sauce on the side.

GARLIC & ONION PASTE

This paste is made especially for my famous Garlic & Onion Brisket (previous page). I like to brush or spoon the paste all over the top and sides of the brisket about 10 to 12 hours before smoking it (or the night before). This allows time to impart a lot of garlic and onion flavors to the meat. I then place the brisket directly on the smoker without rinsing off the paste for a flavor that is out-of-this-world good.

MAKES about 1 cup

---

1 large onion, roughly chopped
8 cloves garlic
¼ cup coarsely ground black pepper
2 Tbsp fresh lemon juice (about
   1 lemon)
¼ tsp cayenne pepper

Combine the ingredients in a food processor or blender and purée to a fine paste.

SMOKED BRISKET FAJITAS

Ever get tired of eating plain smoked brisket? Okay, I don't either, but here is a good way to use leftover brisket in an entirely different way. We really enjoy this recipe as a family, and I find myself smoking a whole brisket specifically for the fajitas. Smoked chicken or pulled pork are also wonderful fajita fillings.

ESTIMATED COOK TIME 20 minutes

SERVES 5

5 Tbsp vegetable oil

2 red bell peppers, julienned

1 small red onion, julienned

1 large jalapeño pepper, seeded and thinly sliced lengthwise

4 cups chopped or pulled smoked brisket (page 104 or 108)

Ten 8-inch flour tortillas

2 cups shredded lettuce

2 cups Perfect Pico de Gallo (page 189)

1 cup sour cream

2 cups shredded cheddar cheese

Heat 3 Tbsp of the oil in a pan set over medium-high heat. Sauté the bell peppers, onion, and jalapeño until soft and the onions are translucent. Add the chopped or pulled brisket and continue to sauté for two more minutes.

Meanwhile, heat the remaining 2 Tbsp of oil in a frying pan set over medium-high heat. Fry the tortillas one at a time until golden brown on both sides, turning once (about 15 seconds per side). Drain on paper towels.

Place the brisket mixture, tortillas, shredded lettuce, pico de gallo, sour cream, and shredded cheddar cheese in separate bowls and allow everyone to build their own fajitas.

PAN-SMOKED BRISKET

While brisket is normally smoked directly on the grate, pan smoking is a method I have been using for a long time to produce a tenderer and juicier brisket, since the meat sits in its own juices while it smokes. I like to flip the brisket a few times during the first half of the smoking session to make sure the smoke flavors both sides of the meat. I must tell you that with this method, due to the steaming effect, the outside of the brisket stays quite tender during the entire process, and very little of the brown crust we call bark forms on the outside of the meat. This is not a problem for me, but it may be a deal-breaker for some.

RECOMMENDED WOOD Mesquite

ESTIMATED COOK TIME 10½ to
   13½ hours (1½ hours per pound)

SERVES 8

7 to 9 lb packer (untrimmed) brisket

2 Tbsp kosher salt

2 Tbsp coarsely ground black pepper

2 Tbsp garlic powder

2 tsp cayenne pepper (optional)

PREPARATION Rinse the brisket under cold water and pat dry with a paper towel. Trim the fat cap so only one-eighth to one-quarter of the fat remains on top of the brisket. Use a sharp knife to make a crosshatch pattern in the remaining fat cap by cutting through the fat down to the meat. This will allow the smoke and heat better access to the meat, and will create a series of pockets to help pool the rendered fat and hold the seasonings in place.

Sprinkle the salt, pepper, and garlic powder over the entire brisket. I recommend a light sprinkling of cayenne pepper for a little added heat, but this can be omitted if desired.

Set the brisket aside for 30 to 45 minutes to allow it to come up to room temperature while you set up your smoker.

SMOKING Prepare your smoker for a long cooking session at 225°F to 240°F. If you are using a gas, an electric, or a charcoal smoker, be sure to have enough wood chips or chunks to produce smoke for about six hours.

Once the smoker is ready, place the prepared brisket in a disposable aluminum pan, fat side up, and set the pan on the smoker grate.

Smoke cook the brisket for about four hours, then flip it fat cap down. Flip the brisket every two hours from that point on to ensure that smoke gets to the entire piece of meat. Also at the four-hour mark, insert a digital probe meat thermometer

(CONTINUED ON PAGE 110)

PAN-SMOKED BRISKET (CONTINUED)

into the side of the brisket so that the thermometer remains intact regardless of whether the meat is fat side up or down.

Once the brisket reaches 160°F, you can tent foil over the top of the pan to help tenderize the meat further and accelerate the cooking process. I usually forego this step unless I am in a hurry.

Once the brisket reaches 195°F, remove it from the smoker. Allow it to rest in the pan for about 30 minutes to give the juices time to redistribute throughout the meat.

FINAL PREPARATION Remove the brisket from the pan and set it aside. Pour the drippings into a lidded container and place in the refrigerator to cool. Once cool, the fat will solidify at the top and can be skimmed off and discarded. What remains is the tasty *jus*, which can be poured over the sliced or pulled brisket to kick up the flavor of the meat.

Slice the brisket into ⅛- to ¼-inch slices or pull it into chunks if you prefer. Serve this juicy rendition of brisket hot with warm barbecue sauce on the side.

BEEF BACK RIBS WITH JEFF'S MOJO

*These are super tasty; however, you will find that most
beef back ribs do not have a lot of meat. Be a little choosy and
hunt for ones that are extra meaty—you'll be a lot happier with
the end result. My mojo recipe (page 144) adds a ton of flavor.*

RECOMMENDED WOOD Oak, hickory,
  or cherry

ESTIMATED COOK TIME 5 hours

SERVES 4 to 6

---

2 racks extra-meaty beef back ribs
  (about 3 to 4 lb per rack)

1 Tbsp kosher salt

1 Tbsp coarsely ground black pepper

2 cups Jeff's Mojo (page 144)

½ cup barbecue sauce (optional)

PREPARATION Rinse the ribs in cold water and pat dry with
a paper towel. Place the ribs on a cutting board bone side up
and remove the membrane (see page 78).

Cut the ribs into individual pieces and lay them in a deep
disposable aluminum pan. Sprinkle the salt and pepper
over the ribs, then pour the Jeff's Mojo overtop. Leave the
ribs on the counter for 30 to 45 minutes to come up to room
temperature while you set up your smoker.

SMOKING Prepare your smoker for cooking at 225°F to 240°F.
If you are using a charcoal, a gas, or an electric smoker, be sure
to have enough wood chips or chunks to produce smoke for
about three hours.

Once the smoker is ready, place the pan of ribs on the
smoker grate and smoke cook for four hours. When this time is
up, remove the ribs from the pan and lay them directly on the
grate for an additional 45 to 60 minutes. This is a good time to
brush on your favorite barbecue sauce if you want to serve the
ribs wet.

When they are tender (see page 15), remove the ribs from
the smoker grate. Place them back in the pan and tent foil over
them to rest for 15 minutes before serving.

RAY'S MEATLOAF

*I started smoking meatloaf many years ago, back when it was
unheard of, and I got a lot of strange looks—even from my wife—
when I first mentioned trying this out. Once folks taste it,
the strange looks change to awe and they are hooked. This is an
excellent version of smoked meatloaf from Ray (Silverwolf636) at
www.smokingmeatforums.com. You could also substitute your
own family meatloaf recipe and smoke it as suggested here.*

RECOMMENDED WOOD Cherry, apple,
   or hickory

ESTIMATED COOK TIME 3 hours

SERVES 6

1½ cups fresh white breadcrumbs

1 lb ground chuck (80/20; see
   page 103)

½ lb plain ground breakfast sausage

6 to 7 medium mushrooms, chopped

1 medium onion, minced

1 large green bell pepper, chopped

3 eggs

1 Tbsp Sriracha sauce (Thai hot chili
   sauce)

1 Tbsp coarsely ground black pepper

1 Tbsp Ray's Deer Rub (page 147)

PREPARATION Prepare the meatloaf at least four hours before
you want to smoke it. This will give the flavors time to saturate
the meat and breadcrumbs.

Preheat the oven to 275°F. Arrange the breadcrumbs in a
single layer on a large cookie sheet and place on the middle
rack of the oven for 20 minutes.

In a large plastic or glass mixing bowl, thoroughly mix the
baked breadcrumbs with the ground chuck, ground breakfast
sausage, mushrooms, onion, bell pepper, eggs, Sriracha sauce,
and pepper. Shape the mixture into a large ball, cover with
plastic wrap, and place in the refrigerator for three hours.

Using a knife or other sharp object, carefully puncture the
bottom of a large 9- × 13-inch disposable aluminum pan with
about one hole per square inch to allow the grease and juices to
drain from the pan.

About one hour before smoking the meatloaf, remove the
ball of meat from the refrigerator. Remove the plastic wrap
and form the meat into a loaf about 4 inches thick inside the
punctured pan. Sprinkle the top of the meatloaf liberally with
Ray's Deer Rub.

Leave the meatloaf on the counter for 20 to 30 minutes to
come up to room temperature while you set up your smoker.

SMOKING Prepare your smoker for cooking at 225°F to 250°F. If you are using a charcoal, a gas, or an electric smoker, make sure to have enough wood chips or chunks to produce smoke for about two hours.

Once the smoker is ready, place the meatloaf pan on the smoker grate. Place a secondary pan below the grate to catch the grease and juices that drain from the meatloaf; this will help keep your smoker clean.

Insert a digital probe meat thermometer at about the one-hour mark to monitor the temperature of the meatloaf. When it reaches 160°F, remove the meatloaf from the smoker, cover it with foil, and let it rest for 15 minutes before slicing and serving.

ABI'S MEATLOAF

This is the meatloaf recipe we use around our house. We used to love it baked in the oven, but now we love it even more smoked. If you have not tried a smoked meatloaf sandwich, you just have to do that soon. A couple of slices of your favorite bread, your favorite condiments, onions, lettuce, and a thick slice of smoked meatloaf: now you're talking!

RECOMMENDED WOOD Mesquite, pecan, or oak

ESTIMATED COOK TIME 3 hours

SERVES 6

---

2 lb ground beef (80/20; see page 103)

1 small onion, finely chopped

½ green bell pepper, finely chopped

2 cloves garlic, minced (optional)

1 cup fresh white breadcrumbs

2 eggs, lightly beaten

¾ cup ketchup

¼ cup whole milk

Dash Tabasco sauce

1 cup ketchup

¼ cup light brown sugar

½ cup barbecue sauce (optional)

PREPARATION Place the ground beef, onion, bell pepper, garlic (if using), breadcrumbs, eggs, ketchup, whole milk, and Tabasco into a large mixing bowl, and mix by hand for five minutes or until everything is well blended. In a disposable aluminum pan, form the mixture into a loaf about 3 to 4 inches thick. Leave the meat loaf on the counter for 20 to 30 minutes to come up to room temperature while you set up your smoker.

SMOKING Prepare your smoker for cooking at 225°F to 250°F. If you are using a charcoal, a gas, or an electric smoker, be sure to have enough wood chips or chunks to produce smoke for about two hours.

Once the smoker is ready, place the pan of meatloaf on the grate. At about the one-hour mark, insert a digital probe meat thermometer so you can monitor the temperature of the meatloaf.

Smoke cook the meatloaf for three hours or until the center reaches 160°F. For added flavor, brush the meatloaf with more ketchup mixed with the brown sugar, or with your favorite barbecue sauce, about 30 minutes before it is done. Slice and serve immediately.

SMOKED FILET MIGNON

This recipe comes from Rob Wyman (RobInNY) from www.smokingmeatforums.com, who says it is a favorite at house parties. I highly recommend buying a tenderloin that is already prepared and ready to slice (i.e., its connective tissue and silverskin have been removed); however, if you have the knowledge and want to save a few bucks, you can buy the whole untrimmed tenderloin and do the work yourself.

RECOMMENDED WOOD Apple, cherry, or hickory

ESTIMATED COOK TIME 3¾ to 5¼ hours (45 minutes per pound)

SERVES 6

---

1 cup (2 sticks) butter

½ cup Original Charlie's Sticky Sauce (or your favorite barbecue sauce)

2 shallots, peeled and coarsely chopped

2 sprigs fresh thyme

25 to 30 fresh chives, finely chopped

5 to 7 lb beef tenderloin (connective tissue and silverskin removed)

6 to 8 unpeeled apples (optional if using a charcoal smoker)

PREPARATION Melt the butter slowly in a small saucepan; do not burn. Mix the Charlie's Sticky Sauce, shallots, and herbs into the butter and keep warm so it does not solidify.

Cut the tenderloin into 2-inch-thick steaks without cutting all the way through the meat (i.e., leave them slightly attached). Place a round glass baking dish upside down inside a large aluminum pan, and lay the partially sliced tenderloin atop the dish so that the pieces fan open, which will allow the smoke better access to the meat.

Baste the tenderloin with about ⅓ cup of the melted butter sauce, then leave it for 20 to 30 minutes to come up to room temperature while you set up your smoker.

SMOKING Prepare your smoker for cooking at 250°F to 275°F. If you are using a gas, an electric, or a charcoal smoker, make sure to have enough wood chips or chunks to produce smoke for at least two to three hours. If you are using a charcoal smoker, also place the whole apples on top of the coals for extra flavor.

Place the pan with the tenderloin on the smoker grate. Insert a digital probe meat thermometer at about the one-hour mark so you can monitor the internal temperature of the meat.

Smoke cook for about 45 minutes per pound, or until the meat has reached a temperature of 130°F (medium-rare), or a higher temperature if you desire more well-cooked meat. Baste the meat once each hour with the remaining melted butter sauce while it is in the smoker.

Once the goal temperature has been reached, remove the tenderloin from the smoker and let it rest 15 to 20 minutes with foil tented over the top. While the meat is resting, you can make a sauce or gravy from the drippings in the bottom of the pan, and serve it on the side of or under the sliced meat.

Keep in mind that the ends of the tenderloin will be cooked more than the center; serve accordingly. Garnish with an edible flower blossom, or with slices of fresh melon, a dollop of sour cream, and a few blueberries.

DUTCH'S SMOKED SHREDDED BEEF ENCHILADAS

*My buddy Earl Dowdle (Dutch) from www.smokingmeatforums.com
sent in this recipe favorite; it is truly delicious and a great way
to do things a little differently with smoked meat. The arm chuck
roast is an excellent alternative to brisket, with less fat and a shorter
cooking time. I suggest you give this one a try.*

RECOMMENDED WOOD Oak,
   mesquite, or pecan
ESTIMATED COOK TIME 6 to 9 hours
   (1½ hours per pound)
SERVES 6 to 8

4 to 6 lb arm chuck roast
1 Tbsp kosher salt
1 Tbsp coarsely ground black pepper
1 Tbsp vegetable oil plus enough to
   oil the baking pan
1 large onion, diced
Two 4 oz cans diced green chilies
2 envelopes (1½ oz each) enchilada
   sauce mix (or two 15 oz cans
   enchilada sauce)
Twenty-four 8-inch flour tortillas
4 cups shredded Colby cheese (or
   Colby-Jack cheese)

PREPARATION Rinse the roast under cold water and pat dry
with a paper towel. Sprinkle the salt and pepper over the entire
roast, then set it aside for 30 to 45 minutes to allow it to come
up to room temperature while you set up your smoker.

SMOKING Prepare your smoker for cooking at 225°F to 240°F.
If you are using a charcoal, an electric, or a gas smoker, be sure
to have enough wood chips or chunks to produce smoke for
about four hours.

Place the roast directly on the smoker grate. At about the
four-hour mark, insert a digital probe meat thermometer
into the thickest part of the roast so you can monitor the
temperature of the meat. Continue smoke cooking for about
one and a half hours per pound (about six to nine hours for
this size roast), or until the internal temperature reaches 180°F.

Once the roast is done cooking, transfer it to the counter
and use two forks to shred the cooked beef. Put the shredded
beef into a large saucepan and set aside.

ASSEMBLING Heat the oil in a frying pan set over medium-
high heat. Sauté the onion until tender, then stir half of the
onion and all of the green chilies into the shredded beef.

Prepare the enchilada sauce mix according to the directions
on the envelopes (or use cans of prepared enchilada sauce). Stir
half of the sauce into the shredded beef mixture to moisten it.

Stir the reserved onion into the remaining sauce. Lightly oil
two 12- × 9-inch baking pans, and evenly coat the bottom of
the pans with half of the onion/enchilada sauce mix.

Fill each tortilla with approximately 3 Tbsp of the beef mixture. Roll and place seam side down in the baking pans, 12 enchiladas per pan. When all are rolled, pour the remaining onion/enchilada sauce mix evenly over the tops of the enchiladas and generously cover with the cheese.

Cover with aluminum foil and bake in the oven at 350°F for 30 to 45 minutes. If using glass baking dishes, reduce the baking time to 20 to 35 minutes, or bake at 325°F for 30 to 45 minutes.

CHERRY-SMOKED PRIME RIB

Smoked prime rib is a staple at our house around the holidays and on really special occasions. You could use a coarse steak seasoning, such as Emeril's Steak Seasoning, in place of the rub. Occasionally spray some sweet cherry juice on the outside of the meat while it cooks, for a nice, subtle cherry-flavoured crust.

RECOMMENDED WOOD Cherry or pecan

ESTIMATED COOK TIME 5 hours

SERVES 6

5 lb prime rib
2 Tbsp kosher salt
2 Tbsp coarsely ground black pepper
2 Tbsp garlic flakes
2 Tbsp minced onion
1 Tbsp red pepper flakes
Spray olive oil
2 cups cherry juice

PREPARATION Use a very sharp knife to make a cut right next to the bone of the prime rib, all the way down to where the feather bones end but not clean through the meat (i.e., leave the meat attached).

Use butcher's twine to tie up the prime rib at ¾-inch intervals all the way along the length of the meat. This keeps the meat from separating during the cooking process and makes for a prettier entrée to serve.

In a small bowl, mix the salt, pepper, garlic flakes, onion, and red pepper flakes together to form a rub. Spray some olive oil on the meat to act as a sticking agent, then sprinkle on the rub. Leave the prime rib on the counter for 30 to 45 minutes to come up to room temperature while you set up your smoker.

SMOKING Prepare your smoker for cooking at about 225°F to 240°F. If you are using a charcoal, an electric, or a gas smoker, make sure you have enough wood chips or chunks to produce about four hours of smoke.

Place the prime rib directly on the smoker grate. Spray the meat with the cherry juice about once every hour. Insert a digital probe meat thermometer into the thickest part of the meat at about the two-hour mark. Prime rib should be cooked only to medium-rare, so be sure to remove the meat from the smoker as soon as it hits 130°F.

Remove the prime rib from the smoker and place it in a pan with foil tented over the top until it is time to eat. The temperature of the meat will rise as much as 5°F to 10°F within 30 minutes.

(CONTINUED ON PAGE 122)

CHERRY-SMOKED PRIME RIB (CONTINUED)

To serve, remove the butcher's twine, then finish the cut right next to the feather bones all the way through the meat. You will be left with solid meat and no bones. Slice the meat into ¾-inch-thick steaks and serve immediately.

TIPS FOR SMOKING
FISH & SEAFOOD

Smoking fish deserves a book all of its own, but a few basics will allow you to do some experimenting. And who knows? Maybe that book on smoking fish will be written soon.

TYPES OF FISH TO SMOKE

Oily fish like salmon, trout, and catfish are the best candidates for smoking. Leaner fish tend to get dry and tough when smoked. You can still try smoking them, but be forewarned.

Whatever fish you choose, make sure it is as fresh as possible and comes from a reputable source.

TYPES OF WOOD TO USE

Alder, oak, apple, pecan, or other mild woods produce the best results when smoking fish.

4

FISH & SEAFOOD

BRINING AND DRYING

I recommend brining both whole fish and fish fillets before smoking; the reaction of the salt and sugar with the flesh of the fish seems to yield a much moister and more flavorful result. The recipes that follow provide detailed brining instructions.

For fish fillets, drying is also crucial to getting that authentic smoked fish taste cherished by so many. Drying keeps the fatty oils on the inside of the fish and stops the moisture from seeping out. While drying, the fish forms a shiny glazed surface that is sticky to the touch. This is known as the pellicle, and it can take from one to two hours to form. Place the fish in a flat pan and refrigerate it while it is drying.

NOT TOO HOT, NOT TOO COLD

Hot smoking is done at temperatures from 200°F to 250°F, while cold smoking is generally done at temperatures less than 90°F. The best results when smoking fish seem to come from somewhere in the middle, from 150°F to 180°F for most fillets, to as hot as 225°F for whole fish.

For oily fillets such as salmon, your smoker should be prepared for cooking at 150°F to 160°F. It is necessary to stay in this range the entire time to prevent the white fat from seeping to the surface. A nice incremental smoking method I use with salmon fillets is to smoke the fish for two hours at 150°F, then at 160°F to finish. When the thickest part of the fish begins to flake, it is done. Non-oily fillets like mahi-mahi or whole fish such as trout can be smoke cooked at 210°F to 225°F.

Be sure to place the fish skin side down on the smoker grate, or use a piece of parchment paper between the fish and the grate to keep the fish from sticking.

LEMON- & ONION-STUFFED WHOLE TROUT

*When I think of smoking fish, what always comes
to mind is trout. The apple smoke that I usually apply
just puts the icing on the cake for a wonderful meal.*

RECOMMENDED WOOD Apple or alder

ESTIMATED COOK TIME 2 hours

SERVES 4

BRINE

1 gallon cold water

1 cup kosher salt

¾ cup lightly packed light brown
  sugar

2 cloves garlic, crushed (optional)

2 Tbsp fresh lemon juice (about
  1 lemon)

FISH

4 whole trout (1 lb fish are the best
  size for individual portions)

1 Tbsp kosher salt

1 Tbsp coarsely ground black pepper

¼ cup (½ stick) butter, sliced in
  4 pieces lengthwise

2 cloves garlic, halved

½ small onion, cut into wedges

1 lemon, cut into wedges

3 to 4 sprigs fresh lemon balm, ends
  trimmed (optional)

PREPARATION To make the brine, place the water into a large plastic container. Add the salt and stir until it is dissolved completely and the water becomes clear again. Add the brown sugar and stir until dissolved. Add the crushed garlic (if using) and lemon juice to complete.

Place the trout into a nonreactive plastic or glass container, and pour enough brine over the fish to cover it completely. Cover and refrigerate for about two hours.

After brining, rinse the trout in cold water and pat dry with a paper towel. Lightly sprinkle the inside of the fish with more salt and the pepper.

To stuff each trout, layer a slice of the butter and one-quarter of each of the garlic, onion, lemon, and lemon balm (if using) into the cavity. Tie loosely with butcher's twine to keep the stuffing from falling out during the smoking process.

Make a foil boat for each fish by folding a 12- × 12-inch piece of foil in half, then in half again so that you end up with a 3- × 12-inch piece of layered foil. Fold over about 1 inch of each end of the long strip, then pull open the center to form a sort of "boat." Place each fish in a foil boat and set aside while you set up your smoker.

SMOKING Prepare your smoker for cooking at 210°F to 225°F. If you are using a charcoal, an electric, or a gas smoker, make sure to have enough smoking wood chips or chunks to produce smoke for about one and a half hours.

Once the smoker is ready, place the foil boats of fish on the grate. Insert a digital probe meat thermometer at about the one-hour mark. Remove the fish as soon as it reaches 145°F or the fish begins to flake (after about two hours). The flesh will also turn slightly opaque when the fish is done. Remove the butcher's twine carefully. Serve the trout in their foil boats.

SMOKED SALMON

*While I do not consider myself an expert on the smoking of fish, I feel
I have mastered salmon. We make it quite often in our home; the
family usually just stands around the kitchen counter grabbing pieces of
the cooked fish. Keep the smoke light and the heat low, and the reward
will be a big smile on your face once you've tasted the result.*

RECOMMENDED WOOD Apple or alder
ESTIMATED COOK TIME 4 to 5 hours
SERVES 4 to 6

BRINE
1 gallon cold water
1 cup kosher salt
¾ cup lightly packed light brown
   sugar
4 cloves garlic, crushed

FISH
3 to 4 lb salmon fillet

PREPARATION Place the water into a large plastic container.
Add the salt and stir until it is dissolved completely and the
water becomes clear again. Add the brown sugar and stir until
dissolved.

Place the salmon fillet into a nonreactive plastic or glass
container and pour enough brine over the fish to cover it
completely. Add the garlic, then cover the container with a lid
or plastic wrap and refrigerate it for about two hours.

After brining, rinse the fish thoroughly with cold water and
pat dry with a paper towel. Allow the surface of the fish to dry
until it forms a pellicle, a tacky surface that helps hold in the
natural juices of the fish. This could take as much as two hours.
I recommend placing the fish in the refrigerator for this process.

Once the pellicle has formed, place the salmon on a piece of
parchment paper that is slightly wider than the fish. Leave the
fish on the counter while you set up your smoker.

SMOKING Prepare your smoker for cooking at 150°F to 160°F.
If you are using a charcoal, an electric, or a gas smoker, make
sure to have enough wood chips or chunks to produce smoke
for about two hours.

Once the smoker is ready, place the salmon with the
parchment paper on the grate. Insert a digital probe meat
thermometer at a 45-degree angle into the thickest part of the
fish so you can monitor the temperature while it cooks. Smoke
cook for about four to five hours, or until the fillet reaches an
internal temperature of 145°F.

Serve the fish as soon as it is done, or let it cool and use it to
make Abi's Salmon and Chive Spread (page 133).

ABI'S SALMON & CHIVE SPREAD

*When I smoke salmon, this is usually how we use up the leftovers.
If you don't brine the salmon before smoking it, you may need to salt
the spread lightly to taste. For an extra-special treat, try the spread
on small pieces of melba toast—my personal favorite!*

MAKES about 2 cups

8 oz pkg cream cheese, softened

¼ cup chopped fresh chives

3 Tbsp fresh lemon juice (about
 1 lemon)

1 tsp ground cumin

1 cup Smoked Salmon (page 130),
 flaked

In a small bowl, combine the cream cheese, chives, lemon juice, and cumin. Fold in the smoked salmon and serve with crackers.

SMOKED MAHI-MAHI

*When I think of mahi-mahi, I think of Hawaii and tropical flavors,
so it only makes sense to smoke this fish with citrus wood, if available,
and finish it with refreshing Pineapple Salsa (page 190). Be sure to
brine the fish before smoking for best results.*

RECOMMENDED WOOD Orange, alder,
or apple

ESTIMATED COOK TIME 2 hours

SERVES 4

BRINE

1 gallon cold water

1 cup kosher salt

¾ cup lightly packed light brown
sugar

¼ cup pineapple, crushed (fresh
or canned)

3 cloves garlic, crushed

FISH

2 lb mahi-mahi fillet

1 Tbsp coarsely ground black pepper

¼ cup Pineapple Salsa (page 190)

PREPARATION Place the water into a large plastic container.
Add the salt and stir until it is dissolved completely and the
water becomes clear again. Add the brown sugar and stir until
dissolved.

Place the mahi-mahi into a nonreactive plastic or glass
container, and pour enough brine over the fish to cover it
completely. Add the pineapple and garlic, cover the container
with a lid or plastic wrap, and refrigerate it for about two hours.

After brining, rinse the fish thoroughly with cold water and
pat dry with a paper towel. Allow the surface of the fish to dry
until it forms a pellicle, a tacky surface that helps hold in the
natural juices of the fish. This could take up to two hours. I
recommend placing the fish in the refrigerator for this process.

Once the pellicle has formed, sprinkle the pepper onto the
fish and place it in a shallow pan. Leave the fish on the counter
while you set up your smoker.

SMOKING Prepare the smoker for cooking at 210°F to 225°F.
If you are using a charcoal, an electric, or a gas smoker, make
sure to have enough wood chips or chunks on hand to produce
smoke for about one hour.

Once the smoker is ready, place the pan of mahi-mahi
on the grate. Insert a digital probe meat thermometer at a
45-degree angle into the thickest part of the fish. Smoke cook
for about two hours, or until the fish reaches an internal
temperature of 145°F.

Cut the mahi-mahi into individual portions of about
4 to 6 ounces, and spoon the Pineapple Salsa over the fish
immediately before serving.

CAJUN-SMOKED FROG LEGS

I know this recipe may be somewhat unconventional, but I have smoked frog legs on several occasions, and they are quite tasty. Be sure to soak them in milk overnight to get rid of any gamey taste before you smoke them. This recipe calls for Cajun seasoning, but you could simplify things by applying only a light dusting of salt and pepper and basting with butter to keep them moist.

RECOMMENDED WOOD Apple, alder, or pecan

ESTIMATED COOK TIME 2 hours

SERVES 4

---

3 lb frog legs

4 cups whole milk

¼ cup extra virgin olive oil

2 Tbsp Cajun seasoning (such as Tony Chachere's Original Creole Seasoning)

¼ cup (½ stick) butter, melted

PREPARATION Soak the frog legs in the milk for at least 24 hours to remove any gamey flavor. When the frog legs are finished soaking, rinse off the milk and pat the legs dry with a paper towel.

Lay the frog legs in a disposable aluminum pan or cookie sheet with about a half inch of space between each leg. Coat the legs generously with the olive oil, then sprinkle each with the Cajun seasoning. Leave the frog legs on the counter while you set up your smoker.

SMOKING Prepare the smoker for cooking at 225°F to 240°F. If you are using a charcoal, an electric, or a gas smoker, make sure to have enough wood chips or chunks to produce smoke for about one and a half hours.

Once the smoker is ready, place the pan of frog legs on the grate. Smoke cook them for about two hours, or until they are tender and the meat easily separates from the bone. About halfway through the cook time, brush the melted butter on the frog legs to keep them from drying out while they cook.

Serve the legs immediately after cooking for best flavor.

TIPS FOR FANTASTIC FLAVOR

WHY USE SAUCES, MARINADES, BRINES, & RUBS

What would smoked meat be without the accompanying sauces and rubs we are all so fond of? I know many folks who say that if you need sauce then the meat is not smoked or cooked correctly. Well, while the meat should be able to stand on its own, I love how complementary barbecue sauces and rubs bring out the special savory flavors of ribs, brisket, steaks, and even fish and poultry.

I think we can all agree that dumping barbecue sauce all over meat does not magically turn it into barbecue. I have seen this maneuver at restaurants, and I just want to scream, "It's fake! Get out while you can!" Sure, I'd be labeled as a madman, but I'm not half as crazy as those who believe that anything other than real smoke and fire can produce real barbecue. Barbecue is so called because of the way it is cooked and the smoke flavor that is imparted in a low-heat, slow-cooking atmosphere. No amount of sauce or rub will ever be able to put that kind of magic into play on a piece of meat.

Now that we have established that . . .

There is a place for all kinds of sauces, marinades, brines, and rubs in a smoking kitchen, and I will show you in this chapter how to use these wonderful concoctions properly to turn what could be ordinary into something quite fantastic!

KICKING UP THE

FLAVOR

MAKING YOUR OWN SAUCES & RUBS

Yes, I said it: you can make your own sauces and rubs and say goodbye forever to the store-bought stuff that just doesn't have that special homemade flavor. This chapter provides several tried-and-true recipes, but I encourage you to step outside the box and experiment with different ingredients to come up with your own homemade blends. Nothing will make you prouder than when someone eats something you created and says, "Man, you ought to bottle this stuff up and sell it!"

For sauce, begin with a little ketchup or a can of stewed tomatoes, and just start adding things you like or that you think sound good. Write down everything you do in a special notebook and keep it handy. Once you try your creation on a piece of meat, you might decide to cut back on the molasses or add a little more Tabasco, and you should note those changes in your book. Over time as you make changes to the recipe, you are bound to develop something really delicious.

The same goes for rubs. Start with ingredients like brown sugar, various ground peppers, paprika, cumin, cinnamon, salt, etc. in varying proportions based on what you think sounds good. Taste and adjust over and over until you come up with something you really like. Keep the salt to a minimum and add only enough to bring out the natural flavors of the other spices. Give the rub a good name and you've got a winner on your hands. Once again, don't trust your memory; be sure to write down everything you do.

If you enjoy using store-bought sauces and rubs, I won't hold it against you. There are tons of choices, and I recommend you be adventurous and try different products until you find the ones you really like and know the ones you can live without.

DRY, LUMPY BROWN SUGAR

Brown sugar is a key ingredient in many rubs, but if your brown sugar looks really dry or lumpy, do *not* throw it away. Put it in the microwave for about 10 to 15 seconds and then check its consistency. Repeat this process three or four times until it is as soft and silky as when it came fresh from the store.

HOW TO STORE DRY RUBS

Dry rubs can be placed in a Ziploc bag and set in the freezer for up to 12 months. This will keep all of the ingredients fresh and in tip-top shape until you are ready to use the rub. For larger quantities, you could also use a plastic container with a tight-fitting lid.

APPLYING RUB TO MEAT

In recent years, my method for applying rub is to allow it to slip through my fingers at a steady pace onto the meat I am preparing, but there is a much easier way. Pour the rub into a plastic bottle with very large holes (like the one you would use for red pepper flakes) and shake the bottle over the meat evenly. Since there is no silicon dioxide or other anti-clumping agent in homemade rub, you may have to whack the bottle against the edge of a counter once in a while to loosen the rub.

A great way to coat smaller pieces of meat with a spice rub is to place the rub with an equal amount of canola or olive oil in a Ziploc bag. Add the meat, close the bag, and shake or roll it to coat the meat. If your meat has a skin (as with poultry), this will get the rub under the skin. It also eliminates the need for a sticking agent, like the mustard called for in many of the recipes in this book.

SLIM'S SWEET & STICKY BARBECUE SAUCE

*This recipe was sent to me by slim at www.smokingmeatforums.com,
and it is just the ticket for wet ribs or brisket, or as a dipping sauce for
chicken nuggets if that's your thing. This recipe is best with the
Famous Dave's sauce, but if you can't find that, you can use as your base
another store-bought sauce that claims to be sweet and/or zesty,
then add the other ingredients to kick it up.*

ESTIMATED COOK TIME 15 minutes

MAKES about 4 cups

1 cup Famous Dave's Sweet & Zesty
   BBQ Sauce

1 cup honey

½ cup (1 stick) butter

½ cup ketchup

¼ cup orange juice

¼ cup light brown sugar

3 Tbsp Dijon mustard

2 Tbsp plain white vinegar

2 Tbsp soy sauce

2 Tbsp coarsely ground black pepper

1 Tbsp chili powder

1 Tbsp garlic powder

Combine all the ingredients in a medium saucepan set over
medium heat. Allow the sauce to simmer lightly for about
15 minutes, stirring often.

Use immediately, or store in a jar or an airtight container in
the refrigerator. Use within three to four weeks for best flavor.

MEMPHIS BARBECUE SAUCE NO. 1

A little sweet and a little savory, with a touch of spicy for that just-right approach to barbecue, this sauce can be painted on ribs about 30 minutes before they are finished to produce sticky ribs, or it can be served warm on the side. It is also delicious on pulled pork sandwiches, or as a dipping sauce for chicken. Feel free to omit the liquid smoke, or take the spiciness up a notch by adjusting the amount of black and cayenne pepper used in the recipe. Special thanks to Blake McCloud (smokeys my pet) at www.smokingmeatforums.com for submitting this recipe.

ESTIMATED COOK TIME 20 minutes

MAKES about 2½ cups

1 Tbsp butter
¼ cup finely chopped onion
1½ cups ketchup
¼ cup chili sauce (I recommend Heinz Chili Sauce)
3 to 4 Tbsp light brown sugar
3 to 4 Tbsp molasses
2 Tbsp yellow mustard
1 Tbsp fresh lemon juice (about ½ lemon)
1 Tbsp Worcestershire sauce
1 Tbsp liquid hickory smoke (optional)
1 tsp chili powder
½ tsp garlic powder (or granulated garlic)
½ tsp table salt
½ tsp coarsely ground black pepper, or to taste
Pinch cayenne pepper, or to taste

Melt the butter in a medium saucepan set over medium heat. Add the onion and slowly sauté until soft and just beginning to turn yellow. Add the remaining ingredients. Simmer for about 15 minutes, adjusting the heat as necessary so the mixture does not come to a boil.

Use the sauce immediately, or cool and store in an airtight container in the refrigerator. Use within three to four weeks for best flavor.

MEMPHIS BARBECUE SAUCE NO. 2

Here's another great Memphis-style sauce to liven up the smoker.
The secret to this recipe is the use of different types of sugars to bring out
the flavors of outdoor smoke cooking. This recipe also calls for a little
liquid smoke, but don't feel obligated to add it if you don't like bottled
smoke flavorings. Special thanks to Kurt Huhner (khuhner)
on www.smokingmeatforums.com for submitting this recipe.

ESTIMATED COOK TIME 1 hour

MAKES about 4½ cups

2 cups ketchup

1 cup water

½ cup apple cider vinegar

5 Tbsp sugar

3 Tbsp light brown sugar

2 Tbsp dark brown sugar

1 Tbsp fresh lemon juice
   (about ½ lemon)

1 Tbsp Worcestershire sauce

1 Tbsp liquid hickory smoke
   (optional)

½ Tbsp coarsely ground
   white pepper

½ Tbsp onion powder

½ Tbsp mustard powder

Combine all the ingredients in a saucepan set over medium-high heat. Cover and bring to a boil, then reduce the heat and simmer until thickened, about one hour.

JEFF'S MOJO

I had heard about the famous Cuban mojo used on meats to bring out those special flavors, but I had never experienced it for myself until I decided to try my hand at making it. I knew that most mojo recipes are unique in many ways, but are also built around a common base of ingredients, so after a lot of tasting and adjusting, this is what I came up with. The first thing I used it on was quail, and it was superb. I later used it on some beef ribs, with equally fantastic results— I had finally found my mojo! I am happy to share this recipe, and sincerely hope you enjoy it as much as my family and I do.

ESTIMATED COOK TIME 5 minutes

MAKES about 1½ cups

⅓ cup extra virgin olive oil

6 cloves garlic, minced

½ onion, minced

¼ cup fresh orange juice (about 1 medium orange)

2 Tbsp fresh lemon juice (about 1 lemon)

2 Tbsp fresh lime juice (about 1 lime)

1 Tbsp honey

1 Tbsp Worcestershire sauce

1 Tbsp jalapeño pepper jelly

1 jalapeño pepper, finely chopped

1 tsp red pepper flakes

1 tsp ground cumin

1 tsp kosher salt

1 tsp coarsely ground black pepper

Heat the oil in a 1- to 2-quart saucepan set over medium heat. Add the minced garlic and cook for about 30 seconds. Add the remaining ingredients and bring to a boil. Remove the mojo from the heat and set aside to cool. Once cool, it can be used right away or stored in an airtight container in the refrigerator for several days.

ASIAN SAUCE

*This Asian-inspired sauce was specifically created for Al's
3-2-1 Asian Ribs (page 87), a recipe sent to me by Al (FMCowboy)
at www.smokingmeatforums.com. However, it could also
be used on chicken or even something like pork steaks to bring a little
Asian flair to the table. This recipe uses Sriracha sauce, which is usually
seen in a red bottle with a green top at most Asian restaurants,
but can also be purchased at almost any grocery store.*

MAKES about 1 cup

¾ cup hoisin sauce
¼ cup honey
1 tsp Sriracha sauce

Add all the ingredients into a small bowl and mix by hand using a fork or a small whisk until well blended. Store unused sauce in a closed jar or container in the refrigerator for three to four months.

ALL-PURPOSE RUB

*Don't let this short list of ingredients fool you into thinking there is
anything short about the flavor of this rub. Sometimes the simplest things
in life are the best, and this holds true for the combination of the three
ingredients used here. Try this with chicken, prime rib, pork chops, steaks,
burgers—almost anything that needs a little boost of flavor. Mix this up in
multiple batches so you have some on hand when you need it.*

MAKES about ⅓ cup

2 Tbsp kosher salt
2 Tbsp coarsely ground black pepper
2 Tbsp garlic powder

Combine all the ingredients into a small Ziploc bag, shake to mix, and keep the rub handy for whatever comes your way. For rub application and storage advice, see pages 34–35.

RAY'S DEER RUB

My friend Ray (Silverwolf636) at www.smokingmeatforums.com loves to hunt deer, and while this rub is especially good on his smoked venison, it is pretty tasty on ribs, chicken breasts, and even fried potatoes or popcorn. This combination of spices and other ingredients magically transforms ordinary food into something quite extraordinary. Throw caution to the wind and sprinkle it on generously for some really great-tasting grub. Special thanks to Ray for submitting this recipe.

MAKES about ½ cup

2 Tbsp paprika

1 Tbsp kosher salt

1 Tbsp sugar

1 Tbsp chili powder

1 Tbsp ground cumin

1 Tbsp granulated garlic

½ Tbsp mustard powder

½ Tbsp coarsely ground black pepper

½ Tbsp cayenne pepper

¼ tsp ground cinnamon

Add all the ingredients into a medium-sized bowl, and use your hands or a fork to mix together. For rub application and storage advice, see pages 34–35.

BIG BALD BBQ RUB

What can I say—this rub recipe was sent to me by my friend Todd (BigBaldBBQ) at www.smokingmeatforums.com, who is six foot two and has a shaved head. Todd spent a long time creating and adjusting this rub to get it just right. He told me that for the longest time the recipe seemed to be missing something, until one day he tried adding lemon pepper. For the first time, it was perfect.

MAKES about 2⅓ cups

1 cup sugar
½ cup paprika
2 Tbsp coarsely ground black pepper
2 Tbsp lemon pepper
2 Tbsp kosher salt
2 Tbsp chili powder
2 Tbsp garlic powder
2 Tbsp onion powder
2 Tbsp cayenne pepper

Add all the ingredients into a medium-sized bowl and use your hands or a fork to mix together. For rub application and storage advice, see pages 34–35.

CHEECH'S JAMAICAN JERK CHICKEN RUB

*Cheech from www.smokingmeatforums.com sent in this recipe, and
I can tell you from firsthand experience that it really does something for
chicken. I recommend you try it on chicken legs, thighs, or quarters.
Put the chicken pieces in a large Ziploc bag, pour in the rub,
and give it a good shake for best results.*

MAKES about ⅓ cup

2 Tbsp kosher salt

1 Tbsp sugar

2 tsp cayenne pepper

2 tsp granulated onion

1 tsp granulated garlic

1 tsp ground allspice

1 tsp ground ginger

1 tsp coarsely ground black pepper

½ tsp ground cinnamon

¼ tsp ground cloves

¼ tsp ground nutmeg

Add all the ingredients into a medium-sized bowl. Use your hands or a fork to mix thoroughly before using. For rub application and storage advice, see pages 34–35.

ASIAN RUB

*This rub was created specifically for Al's 3-2-1 Asian Ribs (page 87),
but it could be used very effectively on chicken or beef ribs for a change
of pace. Apply generously for the greatest effect. The recipe can easily
be doubled if you need a larger portion.*

MAKES about ⅓ cup

2 Tbsp light brown sugar

1 Tbsp Chinese five-spice powder

2 tsp ground ginger

1 tsp garlic powder

1 tsp onion powder

1 tsp kosher salt

½ tsp coarsely ground black pepper

¼ tsp cayenne pepper

Add all the ingredients into a small bowl, and mix together by hand using a small whisk or a fork until the rub is well blended and there are no lumps in the brown sugar. For rub application and storage advice, see pages 34–35.

SPECIAL TURKEY BRINE

The Cajun ingredients in this recipe give this brine some kick. Crab boil—a small bottle or boxed mix of highly concentrated seasoning for seafood like crab, shrimp, and crawfish—is optional, but it adds some of that spicy and wonderful Louisiana flavor I have come to love. It is readily available in the southern United States, but can also be found at online stores such as Amazon.com or at specialty Cajun food stores.

ESTIMATED COOK TIME 20 minutes

MAKES about 1 gallon

1 gallon water

1 cup kosher salt

1 cup sugar

3 Tbsp maple syrup

2 Tbsp Tony Chachere's Original Creole Seasoning (or any Cajun seasoning)

1 Tbsp Zatarain's Concentrated Shrimp and Crab Boil (optional)

Combine the water and salt in a large stockpot set on medium-low heat until the salt is completely dissolved and the water is clear.

Add the remaining ingredients and allow the brine to come to a slow boil. Reduce the heat to low and let the brine simmer for about 15 minutes. Remove the brine from the heat and set aside to cool to room temperature. Place in the refrigerator and let it cool further to 39°F before using. For more on how to brine, see pages 37–40.

JEFF'S CAJUN POULTRY BRINE

I love using this all-purpose poultry brine, and it smells really nice while it simmers on the stove. This recipe is the result of me trying to come up with something a little different. I use the Zatarain's Concentrated Shrimp and Crab Boil if I'm in the mood for Cajun-style turkey; otherwise, I leave it out.

ESTIMATED COOK TIME 20 minutes

MAKES about 2½ gallons

2 gallons water

2 cups kosher salt

3 cups sugar

¼ cup Zatarain's Concentrated Shrimp and Crab Boil (optional)

¼ cup coarsely ground black pepper

1 Tbsp dried rosemary leaves

1 Tbsp dried thyme leaves

¼ cup molasses

¼ cup white wine (not cooking wine)

¼ cup Worcestershire sauce

Combine the water and salt in a stockpot large enough to hold at least 3 gallons of water. Set on medium-low heat until the salt is completely dissolved and the water is clear.

Add the remaining ingredients. Allow the brine to simmer over low heat for about 15 minutes without boiling. Remove the brine from the heat and set aside to cool to room temperature. Place the brine in the refrigerator to cool further to 39°F before using. For more on how to brine, see pages 37–40.

JEFF'S TURKEY LEG BRINE

I created this brine recipe especially for turkey legs. The red pepper flakes, Cajun seasoning, and Tabasco sauce really give it a special zing and take the turkey legs you're used to eating to the next level of flavor. Simmering allows the oils from the red pepper flakes to leach into the brine. Feel free to simmer longer if you want a stronger flavor.

ESTIMATED COOK TIME 20 minutes

MAKES about 1 gallon

1 gallon water

1 cup kosher salt

¾ cup lightly packed light brown sugar

2 Tbsp garlic powder

2 Tbsp onion powder

2 Tbsp red pepper flakes

2 Tbsp Cajun seasoning (such as Tony Chachere's Original Creole Seasoning)

2 Tbsp Tabasco sauce

1 Tbsp poultry seasoning

Place the water in a large stockpot set over medium-high heat. Add the salt and stir until it is dissolved completely and the water is clear.

Add the remaining ingredients and allow the brine to come to a slow boil before turning the heat down to low. Let the brine simmer for about 15 minutes. Remove the brine from the heat and set aside to cool to room temperature. Once cooled, place the brine in the refrigerator to cool further to at least 39°F. For more on how to brine, see pages 37–40.

MOP FOR BEEF OR PORK

Many folks feel that you do not gain anything from spritzing or brushing a mop onto meat while it is in the smoker, but I have to disagree. Some of this sugary mixture will adhere to the meat and begin to caramelize in the heat for added layers of flavor. Be sure to apply the mop quickly so as not to hold the door of the smoker open any longer than necessary; about once per hour is plenty.

MAKES about 2 cups

1 cup Dr Pepper
⅔ cup low-sodium soy sauce
⅓ cup extra-virgin olive oil

Add the ingredients to a plastic spray bottle for spritzing meat as it smokes. A few quick sprays every time you open the smoker, or about once every hour, will do wonders for brisket, ribs, pork shoulder, and other meats. Be sure to shake the bottle well before each use to emulsify the oil into the mixture. Store leftovers in the refrigerator in an airtight container. Use within seven days for best flavor.

APPLE BUTTER MOP

Apple-flavored butter sprayed onto meat while it cooks not only sounds good, but tastes great. You can put this mop in a small spray bottle for easier application, or brush it onto the meat about once each hour or whenever you open the door of the smoker to add wood or turn the meat. This mop is particularly good on ribs and smoked chicken breasts.

MAKES about 1½ cups

½ cup (1 stick) butter
1 cup apple juice (or apple cider)

Melt the butter in the microwave. Add the apple juice and whisk together until well blended. For easiest application, pour the mop into a small plastic spray bottle so it can be spritzed onto the meat as it cooks. Microwave for a few seconds and shake to mix the ingredients before each use.

JEFF'S MOP WATER

Okay, it's a funny name, I admit that, but that's what I started calling this concoction, and the name stuck. Although it's just water, butter, and seasoning, it's fantastic on almost any cut of beef—especially brisket. Applying this mop to brisket every hour or so adds tremendous flavor to the outside of the meat and keeps it nice and moist while it cooks. The butter is quick to solidify in the water, so keep the mop warm or microwave it for 20 to 30 seconds and remix it before each use.

MAKES about 1½ cups

1 cup water

½ cup (1 stick) butter

2 Tbsp Cajun seasoning
(I recommend Tony Chachere's
Original Creole Seasoning)

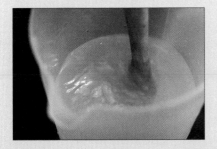

Place the ingredients in a microwaveable dish and microwave until the butter is melted. Keep the mop warm and mix well before each use. Apply with a brush to the top, bottom, and sides of meat as it smokes.

Smoked meats are always the main attraction at our table. However, they wouldn't be the same without delicious sides that perfectly complement the smoked flavors. In this chapter, I've shared a collection of favorite family recipes and a few special contributions from friends.

6

SIDES

ABI'S SUMMER SUCCOTASH

My wife sautés fresh squash and zucchini every year as soon as they are in season. Her grandmother made simple succotash with fresh corn and lima beans, and this is a heartier take on that simple dish. The yellow squash and zucchini go into the dish unpeeled, so be sure to wash them thoroughly before slicing.

ESTIMATED COOK TIME 20 to 25 minutes

SERVES 8

4 strips bacon

1 small red onion, chopped

2 cloves garlic, minced

16 oz bag frozen lima beans, rinsed in cold water and drained

16 oz bag frozen corn, rinsed in cold water and drained (or 2 cups fresh corn cut from the cob)

2 small yellow summer squash (unpeeled), sliced into medallions

1 small zucchini (unpeeled), sliced into medallions

Salt and coarsely ground black pepper to taste

In a large cast iron pan, fry the bacon over medium heat until crisp. When cooked, drain the bacon on paper towels. Remove all but 2 Tbsp of the bacon fat from the pan and set aside in case it's needed later.

Add the onion and garlic to the remaining 2 Tbsp of hot grease, and sauté until the onion softens, about three to four minutes. Add the lima beans, corn, squash, and zucchini, and stir well. Sauté until the vegetables are tender, about 15 to 20 minutes. Add more bacon fat during cooking if necessary. Season with salt and pepper to taste, and crumble the fried bacon on top just before serving.

SMOKE-ROASTED ASPARAGUS

I'm a big fan of asparagus, so I had to add at least one recipe that features this vegetable on the smoker. Balsamic vinegar gives it a nice tang that I think you will enjoy. Make sure to watch the asparagus carefully so you don't overcook it; it should be a bit crisp when you bite into it. This recipe was sent to me by my friend Rob Wyman (RobInNY) at www.smokingmeatforums.com.

RECOMMENDED WOOD Pecan or apple

ESTIMATED COOK TIME 1 hour

SERVES 6

2 to 3 lb fresh asparagus

1 Tbsp kosher salt (approx)

Balsamic vinegar (enough to partially cover the asparagus)

½ cup (1 stick) butter, melted

PREPARATION Snap off the tough ends of the asparagus spears, and use only the tender stalks. Place the asparagus stalks parallel to each other in a shallow pan, season with the kosher salt, and add enough balsamic vinegar to partially cover the stalks.

SMOKING Prepare your smoker for cooking at 225°F to 240°F. If you are using a gas, an electric, or a charcoal smoker, make sure to have enough wood chips or chunks on hand to produce smoke for about one hour.

Place the pan with the asparagus in the smoker for one hour. Do not overcook; the asparagus should be al dente (tender-crisp). Drain off the liquid in the pan after removing from the smoker, and toss the asparagus with the melted butter.

BACON-WRAPPED CHEESE-STUFFED JALAPEÑOS

*Affectionately dubbed "ABTs" (atomic buffalo turds) at
www.smokingmeatforums.com, these stuffed jalapeño peppers
will disappear as quickly as you serve them. Each jalapeño is only a bite
or two, and it's hard to stop taking bites. To make the jalapeños less
spicy, simply seed and devein them as usual, then soak them for 24 hours
in Sprite. You'll still get all the flavor, but with very low heat. Save the
jalapeño-flavored Sprite for use as a mop on pulled pork or brisket.*

*If you have any cream cheese filling left over, spread it onto a flour
tortilla, top with shredded chicken, roll up, and cut into pinwheels.*

RECOMMENDED WOOD Mesquite,
pecan, or oak

ESTIMATED COOK TIME 3 hours

SERVES 6 to 8

---

8 oz pkg cream cheese, softened

1 cup shredded cheddar cheese
(or Colby-Jack cheese)

½ cup thinly sliced green onions

8 jalapeño peppers, seeded and
split lengthwise

8 strips thinly sliced bacon,
chopped in half

PREPARATION In a medium bowl, combine the cream cheese, cheddar, and green onions with a large fork until evenly mixed. Stuff a jalapeño half with about 2 Tbsp of the cheese mixture (or enough to fill the pepper completely). Wrap the stuffed pepper with a half-slice of the bacon, overlapping the bacon on one end, and secure tightly with a toothpick. Place on a baking sheet or rack. Repeat with the remaining jalapeño halves.

SMOKING Prepare your smoker for cooking at 225°F to 240°F. If you are using a charcoal, an electric, or a gas smoker, be sure to have enough wood chips or chunks on hand to produce smoke for about three hours.

Once the smoker is ready, place the stuffed peppers directly on the grate with about a ½ inch between each pepper. Smoke for three hours or until the bacon is crisp and the jalapeños are tender.

BACON-WRAPPED BOUDIN-STUFFED JALAPEÑOS

My oldest daughter says these are irresistible. I couldn't agree more.
Smoked boudin (page 99) is already slightly spicy, so stuffing it into
jalapeño peppers doubles the impact. Make sure that the pepper
and boudin are wrapped tightly with the bacon to prevent them
from drying out during cooking.

RECOMMENDED WOOD Mesquite,
   pecan, or oak
ESTIMATED COOK TIME 3 hours
SERVES 6 to 8

1 lb smoked boudin sausages
   (page 99)
¼ cup beef broth
½ cup thinly sliced green onions
8 jalapeño peppers, split lengthwise
   and seeded
8 strips thinly sliced bacon,
   chopped in half
1 cup barbecue sauce (optional)

PREPARATION Remove the casings from the boudin sausages and place the filling in a medium bowl. Mash the boudin with a fork, then gradually add the beef broth just until moistened. Fold in the green onions. Stuff a jalapeño half with about 2 Tbsp of the boudin mixture. Wrap the pepper with a half-slice of the bacon, overlapping the bacon on one end. Secure tightly with a toothpick, and place on a baking sheet or rack. Repeat with the remaining jalapeños.

SMOKING Prepare your smoker for cooking at 225°F to 240°F. If you are using a charcoal, an electric, or a gas smoker, be sure to have enough wood chips or chunks on hand to produce smoke for about three hours.

Once the smoker is ready, place the stuffed peppers directly on the grate with about a ½ inch between each pepper. Smoke for three hours or until the bacon is crisp and the jalapeños are tender. Brush with your favorite barbecue sauce for the last 10 minutes of cook time, if desired.

BACON-WRAPPED TEX-MEX-STUFFED JALAPEÑOS

Southwest flavors emerge with the addition of fresh corn and cilantro.
These go great with Smoked Brisket Fajitas (page 106).

RECOMMENDED WOOD Mesquite, pecan, or oak

ESTIMATED COOK TIME 3 hours

SERVES 6 to 8

8 oz pkg cream cheese, softened

1 cup shredded cheddar cheese (or Colby-Jack cheese)

½ cup chopped fresh cilantro

½ cup fresh corn, cut from the cob (or ½ cup frozen corn)

8 jalapeño peppers, seeded and split lengthwise

8 strips thinly sliced bacon, chopped in half

PREPARATION In a medium bowl, combine the cheeses, cilantro, and corn. Stuff a jalapeño half with about 2 Tbsp of the cheese mixture (or enough to fill the pepper completely). Wrap the stuffed pepper with a half-slice of the bacon, overlapping the bacon on one end, and secure tightly with a toothpick. Place on a baking sheet or rack. Repeat with the remaining jalapeños.

SMOKING Prepare your smoker for cooking at 225°F to 240°F. If you are using a charcoal, an electric, or a gas smoker, be sure to have enough wood chips or chunks on hand to produce smoke for about three hours.

Once the smoker is ready, place the stuffed peppers directly on the grate with about a ½ inch between each pepper. Smoke for three hours or until the bacon is crisp and the jalapeños are tender.

FIRE CORN

This creamy, spicy corn is a great complement to a rack of baby backs or sliced brisket. Thanks for this recipe go to Bill (Bill in MN) of www.smokingmeatforums.com, who says this is a family favorite.

ESTIMATED COOK TIME 40 to
 45 minutes

SERVES 6

¼ cup (½ stick) butter, melted

¼ cup cornmeal

10½ oz can creamed corn

10½ oz can corn niblets

2 eggs, beaten

2 cups shredded cheddar cheese

4 oz can diced green chilies, drained
 (or, for extra heat, ¼ cup minced
 jalapeño peppers)

⅛ tsp garlic powder

⅛ tsp cayenne pepper

¼ tsp table salt

½ tsp coarsely ground black pepper

Place the melted butter in a large bowl. Add the cornmeal and stir until well combined. Mix in the remaining ingredients and pour into a lightly greased glass baking dish. Bake, uncovered, at 350°F for 40 to 45 minutes. Check doneness after 40 minutes; it should be firm to the touch.

SMOKED CORN ON THE COB

Smoked corn in the husks brings a rustic appeal to the dinner table,
and the smoking process makes sweet corn even sweeter.

RECOMMENDED WOOD Hickory,
  mesquite, or pecan
ESTIMATED COOK TIME 1½ hours
SERVES 6 to 8

6 to 8 ears of corn (husks on)
¼ cup extra virgin olive oil
1 tsp kosher salt
1 tsp coarsely ground black pepper
½ cup (1 stick) butter, softened
1 tsp finely chopped fresh chives

PREPARATION Pull the husks down without removing them from the corncobs. Remove as much of the silk as possible from the corn, then submerge the cobs in a deep pot of cold water so only the green husks are sticking out of the water. Let the corncobs soak for two hours, then remove them from the water and pat them dry with a paper towel.

Mix together the olive oil, salt, and pepper. Rub this mixture all over each corncob, then pull the husks back up to their original position. Don't worry if the husks don't completely cover the corn, since you want some smoke to get to the kernels.

SMOKING Prepare your smoker for cooking at 225°F to 240°F. If you are using a charcoal, an electric, or a gas smoker, be sure to have enough wood chips or chunks on hand to produce smoke for about one and a half hours.

Once the smoker is ready, place the corncobs directly on the grate, leaving a little space between the ears to allow the smoke to access all sides of the corn. When the corn has been smoking for 30 minutes, mix together the butter and chives and rub some of the mixture on the corn, getting it under the husks as well as you can. Repeat this buttering process every 30 minutes until the corn is finished cooking, about one and a half hours in total. Remove the ears from the smoker grate and serve immediately.

GARLIC MASHED POTATOES

My wife, Abi, has certainly mastered the art of making mashed potatoes that are perfectly creamy without being overly gooey. She says it's all about mashing them while they are still very hot. This recipe gives her wonderful mashed potatoes a garlic flavor with oven-roasted garlic cloves. You're going to like this one, I guarantee it!

ESTIMATED COOK TIME 1 hour

SERVES 4 to 6

1 bulb garlic

Cooking spray (or 1 Tbsp vegetable oil)

2½ lb red potatoes or new potatoes, peeled and quartered

1 tsp salt

¼ cup (½ stick) butter

½ tsp salt

½ tsp coarsely ground black pepper

¼ to ⅓ cup heavy cream (35% milk fat)

Preheat the oven to broil. Slice off the top portion of the garlic bulb so the cloves are visible and the top is flat. Spray the bulb lightly with the cooking spray, or brush with vegetable oil, then wrap the bulb in foil and place on a baking sheet. Broil for five minutes. Remove the foil and broil for one to two minutes longer. Remove the garlic from the oven and cool to room temperature.

Place the potatoes in a stockpot with enough water to cover them, and set over medium-high heat. Add the salt and bring to a rolling boil, then reduce heat to medium-low and simmer until the potatoes are easily pricked with a fork (about 20 to 30 minutes).

Remove potatoes from heat and drain in a colander, then return them to the pot. Working quickly while the potatoes are still very hot, grasp the roasted garlic bulb at the bottom and squeeze the cloves into the pot with the potatoes. Discard the bulb. Add the butter, more salt, and the pepper, and roughly mash with a fork or potato masher until thoroughly combined and the butter is melted. (Do not beat with a hand mixer or beater, especially once the potatoes have cooled, as this will result in gooey, sticky potatoes.) Add the heavy cream a little at a time, and mix well until the potatoes are the desired consistency. Serve immediately.

TRIPLEBQ MASHED POTATOES

*Traditional mashed potatoes get a new twist with barbecue
seasoning, crisp bits of bacon, and garlic. Try these with sliced
Garlic and Onion Brisket (page 104) and Abi's Summer Succotash
(page 160). You can substitute any brand of barbecue seasoning
(like McCormick) if you can't find the KC Masterpiece label.
Special thanks to tripleBQ from www.smokingmeatforums.com
for sharing this recipe with us.*

ESTIMATED COOK TIME 25 to
  30 minutes
SERVES 8

3 Tbsp + 2 tsp barbecue seasoning
  (such as KC Masterpiece BBQ
  Seasoning)
3 lb new or red potatoes, peeled and
  quartered
1 lb smoked bacon, chopped into
  small pieces
2 tsp minced garlic
½ cup (1 stick) butter
1½ cups whole milk
Kosher salt and coarsely ground
  black pepper to taste

Bring a large pot of water and 3 Tbsp of the barbecue seasoning to a boil over high heat. Add the potatoes and reduce the heat to medium. Boil for 20 to 25 minutes or until the potatoes are tender. Remove from the heat and drain in a colander. Transfer potatoes to a bowl and mash them immediately, while still very hot.

While the potatoes are boiling, fry the bacon in a frying pan over medium heat until crisp. Drain on paper towels. Sauté the minced garlic in the bacon fat for one to two minutes; remove from the pan with a slotted spatula and set aside.

Add the butter, milk, and the remaining 2 tsp of barbecue seasoning to the mashed potatoes. Stir in the fried bacon and the sautéed garlic, and season with salt and pepper.

CHRISTI'S CHEESY TATERS

*This simple and satisfying potato dish can be whipped up in a
hurry using a bag of frozen potatoes. These go especially well with
smoked meatloaf (pages 112 and 115). Thanks to Todd (BigBaldBBQ)
at www.smokingmeatforums.com for sharing this recipe with us.*

ESTIMATED COOK TIME 1 to 1½ hours

SERVES 8

24 oz bag frozen shredded potatoes
10½ oz can cream of chicken soup
2 cups shredded cheddar cheese
1 cup sour cream
½ cup (1 stick) butter, softened
½ cup onion flakes
1 tsp table salt
½ tsp coarsely ground black pepper

Combine all ingredients in a large bowl and mix well.
Spread into a lightly greased 9- × 9-inch casserole dish.
Bake uncovered in the oven at 350°F for one to one and
a half hours, or until bubbly and browned.

SMOKED POMMES DE TERRE

Some folks have no doubt been smoking potatoes for years, but I found out this is a tasty thing to do quite by accident. I always insert a digital probe meat thermometer into a small potato set on the grate of my smoker so I have an accurate reading of the smoker temperature. When done cooking, I used to just toss the potato over the fence for the cows. But one day I took a bite of the potato on a whim, and it was surprisingly good! I've been eating them ever since, and I now put even more potatoes in the smoker to serve with the rest of the meal. This particular method comes to us from my friend Rob Wyman (RobInNY) at www.smokingmeatforums.com.

RECOMMENDED WOOD Mesquite or hickory

ESTIMATED COOK TIME 3 hours

SERVES 6 to 8

6 to 8 russet potatoes
¼ cup vegetable oil

PREPARATION Wash the potatoes and rub the skin of each one with the oil. Pierce each potato with a fork twice on the same side.

SMOKING Prepare your smoker for cooking at 225°F to 240°F. If you are using a gas, an electric, or a charcoal smoker, make sure to have enough wood chips or chunks on hand to produce smoke for about three hours.

Once the smoker is ready, place the potatoes pierced side up on the grate, and bake until soft and mushy inside (about three hours; the potato should feel tender when you squeeze it lightly). The potatoes will be very hot, so handle them with care. Serve hot, either unopened or "flowered" by slicing the skin and squeezing the potato flesh from the ends and upward from the bottom.

TRADITIONAL BAKED BEANS

*There's nothing like good old-fashioned baked beans, and because these
are made in a slow cooker, there's no need to soak them ahead of time.*

ESTIMATED COOK TIME 13 to 14 hours

SERVES 6 to 8

4½ cups water

1 lb dried small white beans, rinsed

½ lb bacon, chopped into small
pieces

½ cup mild-flavored molasses
(blackstrap is also fine, but will
result in a stronger taste)

½ cup lightly packed light brown
sugar

1 onion, chopped

⅓ cup ketchup

2 Tbsp Dijon mustard

½ tsp table salt

½ tsp liquid hickory smoke

Combine all the ingredients in a slow cooker. Cover and cook
on the low setting for 13 to 14 hours or until beans are soft.
For best results, stir the beans two to three times while they
cook, but do this quickly to reduce unnecessary heat loss.

DUTCH'S WICKED BAKED BEANS

These beans will make even "chili heads" happy. You can increase the heat in this recipe by chopping the jalapeños with the seeds in, but be careful about serving it this way to those with sensitive palates, especially children or the elderly. To make these beans family friendly, omit the jalapeños and the mustard powder. If you are making this as a side dish for Smoked Pork Spare Ribs (page 79), start cooking the beans when the ribs have three hours left to cook. You can smoke the removed flap of meat from the ribs for one to one and a half hours, then dice the meat and stir it into the beans before placing them in the smoker.

RECOMMENDED WOOD Mesquite, pecan, or oak

ESTIMATED COOK TIME 2½ to 3 hours

SERVES 8

6 to 8 strips bacon, chopped into ½-inch pieces

½ medium onion, diced

½ green bell pepper, diced

1 to 2 jalapeño peppers, seeded and diced

55 oz can (or two 28 oz cans) Bush's Original Baked Beans (or any brand you prefer)

8 oz can crushed pineapple, drained

1 cup light brown sugar, packed

1 cup ketchup

1 Tbsp mustard powder

PREPARATION Sauté the bacon pieces in a frying pan over medium heat until crispy; remove from pan with a slotted spoon. Add the onion, bell pepper, and jalapeños to the same pan and sauté until tender, about five minutes.

Combine the remaining ingredients in a large mixing bowl. Stir in the sautéd bacon pieces and vegetables. If the mixture looks dry, add additional ketchup, ¼ to ½ cup at a time. Pour the whole contents into a 12- × 9-inch, or a deep 9- × 9-inch, aluminum baking pan.

SMOKING Prepare your smoker for cooking at 220°F to 250°F. If you are using a charcoal, a gas, or an electric smoker, be sure to have enough wood chips or chunks to produce smoke for about three hours.

Once the smoker is ready, place the pan of beans on the grate and smoke cook for two and a half to three hours. (Alternatively, you can cover the beans with foil and bake in a 350°F oven for one hour.) If you are smoking ribs or other meat above the beans so that the tasty juices can drip down, place an instant-read thermometer into the beans without touching the pan to make sure the temperature of the beans reaches at least 160°F.

GARY'S FAMOUS OYSTER STUFFIN' MUFFINS

This is a clever way to serve individual portions of oyster stuffing at Thanksgiving (or any other time you're in the mood for turkey, stuffing, and cranberry sauce). Special thanks to my friend Gary (iGolf2) at www.smokingmeatforums.com for creating this excellent recipe and sharing it with us.

ESTIMATED COOK TIME 45 minutes

SERVES 10 to 12

1 Tbsp butter

1 stalk celery, finely chopped

½ large onion, finely chopped

6 slices white bread, lightly toasted and cubed

6 slices whole wheat bread, lightly toasted and cubed

¾ cup chicken broth

1 egg

½ tsp garlic powder

1 tsp kosher salt

1 tsp coarsely ground black pepper

12 freshly shucked oysters

Melt the butter in a small saucepan. Add the celery and onion and sauté until soft.

In a large mixing bowl, combine the white and whole wheat toast cubes, sautéed celery and onion, chicken broth, egg, garlic powder, salt, and pepper. Add more chicken broth or toast cubes to achieve the desired consistency, which is moist but not soggy or runny.

Lightly grease each cup of a regular muffin tin and preheat the oven to 350°F.

Spoon the mixture into each muffin cup to about two-thirds full. Use your thumb to make a small bowl shape in the top of the mixture, then place a shucked oyster in each "bowl." Top the muffins with more batter until full.

Bake the stuffin' muffins in the preheated oven for about 45 minutes, or until the muffin tops are golden brown.

MOINK BALLS

The most amazing things can sometimes be the simplest—like these tasty and easy-to-make morsels. Part beef (moo!), part bacon (oink!), the name "moink balls" has stuck. Larry Gaian from TheBbqGrail.com invented these for a wedding, and they have since become quite the novelty. If you're in a pinch, you could use frozen beef or Italian meatballs instead of making your own.

RECOMMENDED WOOD Mesquite, pecan, or oak

ESTIMATED COOK TIME 2 hours

SERVES 8

2 lb ground chuck or ground beef (80/20; see page 103)

½ cup fresh white breadcrumbs

2 eggs

1 Tbsp kosher salt

1 Tbsp coarsely ground black pepper

½ Tbsp garlic powder

3 Tbsp Worcestershire sauce

1 Tbsp Frank's RedHot Original Cayenne Pepper Sauce

1 lb thinly sliced bacon, chopped in half

Jalapeño or habañero pepper jelly, or barbecue sauce (optional)

PREPARATION Combine the ground chuck or beef, breadcrumbs, eggs, salt, pepper, garlic powder, Worcestershire sauce, and Frank's RedHot in a large mixing bowl, and mix until well blended. Using your hands, form twenty-four 1-inch meatballs.

Wrap a half-slice of the bacon around each meatball and secure with a toothpick inserted all the way through the ball.

SMOKING Prepare your smoker for cooking at 225°F to 240°F. If you are using a charcoal, an electric, or a gas smoker, be sure to have enough wood chips or chunks on hand to produce smoke for about two hours.

Once the smoker is ready, place the meatballs directly on the grate. Smoke cook for two hours or until the bacon is crispy. About 30 minutes before the meatballs are finished cooking, apply an optional glaze of hot pepper jelly or your favorite barbecue sauce. Serve immediately after removing from the smoker.

ABI'S CLASSIC POTATO SALAD

This is my wife's recipe, which is a happy marriage of traditional potato salad and her grandma's German potato salad. It goes great with Smoked Pork Spare Ribs (page 79) or Smoked Chicken Quarters (page 59). We also serve it with Smoked Chicken Gumbo with Andouille (page 75) in true Cajun style: place a dollop of the potato salad in a bowl and ladle a serving of gumbo over the top.

ESTIMATED COOK TIME 30 minutes

SERVES 12

½ lb bacon

2½ lb potatoes, peeled and cut into ½-inch cubes

3 hard-boiled eggs, cooled and chopped

½ cup finely chopped dill pickles

½ cup finely chopped green olives (optional)

1 large red onion, finely chopped

½ cup mayonnaise

2 Tbsp yellow mustard

Table salt and coarsely ground black pepper to taste

Sauté the bacon in a frying pan over medium heat until crispy; remove from the pan with a slotted spoon and set on paper towel to drain and cool. Crumble into small pieces and set aside.

Bring a large pot of lightly salted water to a boil. Add the potatoes and reduce heat to medium. Simmer just until tender, but not mushy, about 20 minutes. Drain and cool without stirring. Place the cooled potatoes in a large bowl and fold in the eggs, pickles, olives (if using), and onion, being careful not to mash the potatoes.

In a separate small bowl, whisk together the mayonnaise and mustard, and fold this into the potato mixture. Add salt and pepper to taste, and top with the crumbled bacon just before serving.

MEXICAN CORN SALAD

This is my sister-in-law P. J.'s recipe, and it's a great complement to smoked fish or chicken. The southwestern flavors are at their best if you can use all fresh ingredients. If using fresh corn instead of canned or frozen, cut it off the cobs and blanch for about five minutes before mixing it into the salad. Enjoy!

SERVES 6

Two 10½ oz cans corn, drained (or one 16 oz bag frozen corn, rinsed in a colander with warm water)
1 medium ripe tomato, chopped
½ red onion, finely chopped
½ cup chopped fresh cilantro
Table salt and coarsely ground black pepper to taste

Toss all ingredients together in a large bowl, cover, and refrigerate for at least two hours before serving.

CLASSIC CREAMY COLESLAW

*Another of my wife's recipes, this creamy slaw is great
on pulled pork sandwiches (see page 82).*

SERVES 8

DRESSING
½ cup mayonnaise
2 Tbsp heavy cream (35% milk fat)
1 tsp fresh lemon juice
¼ tsp celery seed (optional)
1 tsp sugar
¼ tsp sea salt
¼ tsp coarsely ground black pepper

SLAW
4 cups shredded green cabbage
1 cup shredded carrots
½ cup shredded red cabbage
  (optional)

In a small bowl, whisk together the mayonnaise, heavy cream, lemon juice, celery seed (if using), sugar, salt, and pepper. Taste and add more salt if necessary.

Combine and toss the green cabbage and carrots together in a large bowl. Pour the dressing over the cabbage mixture and toss to coat. Cover and refrigerate for at least two hours. If using the shredded red cabbage, add just before serving; otherwise, all the ingredients will be tinted purple.

SPICY CLASSIC CREAMY COLESLAW

Classic Creamy Coleslaw (above) gets a kick from spices and peppers.

1 small onion, grated
2 jalapeño peppers, seeded and
  minced
2 Tbsp ground cumin
½ tsp Tabasco sauce
¼ tsp cayenne pepper

To the Classic Creamy Coleslaw dressing (above), add the grated onion, jalapeños, cumin, Tabasco, and cayenne, and toss with the slaw ingredients.

TANGY COLESLAW

Some folks like coleslaw to be sweet, while others prefer theirs on the tangy side. If the latter is what you're looking for, you will be sure to like this recipe. Capers add a flavor profile that will excite your senses—and that's saying a lot for a dish that's almost never in the spotlight.

SERVES 8

DRESSING
¾ cup mayonnaise
1 tsp white wine vinegar
¼ tsp sea salt
½ tsp coarsely ground black pepper

COLESLAW
4 cups shredded green cabbage
1 cup shredded carrots
1 small Vidalia onion, grated
3 Tbsp capers

Whisk together the mayonnaise, white wine vinegar, salt, and pepper. Combine the cabbage, carrots, onion, and capers in a large bowl. Add the dressing and toss to coat. Chill in the refrigerator until ready to serve.

RANGECOP'S RED CABBAGE SLAW WITH MARINATED RED ONIONS

This tangy slaw, contributed by Rangecop, a member of www.smokingmeatforums.com, pairs perfectly with Smoked Duck with Wine Butter Sauce (page 68). You'll have extra onions, which you can save to make more slaw, top a burger, or, if you're a die-hard onion fan like me—just eat by themselves.

SERVES 8

MARINATED ONIONS

¼ cup apple cider vinegar

1 Tbsp chopped fresh tarragon
 (or 1 tsp dried tarragon leaves)

¼ tsp sea salt

Coarsely ground black pepper
 to taste

½ cup canola oil

2 large red onions, thinly sliced

SLAW

4 cups shredded red cabbage

2 cups shredded carrots

3 Tbsp chopped sweet pickles

DRESSING

⅓ cup apple cider vinegar

½ cup canola oil

2 Tbsp sugar

1 tsp Creole mustard (or
 grainy mustard)

½ tsp sea salt

Coarsely ground black pepper
 to taste

To make the marinated onions, combine the vinegar, tarragon, salt, and pepper in a small bowl. Whisk in the oil. Pour over the sliced onions and refrigerate overnight in a lidded glass container. This makes about 2 cups.

To make the slaw, combine the cabbage, carrots, pickles, and ½ cup of the marinated onions (you'll have some left over) in a large bowl and toss.

For the dressing, combine the vinegar, oil, sugar, and mustard in a small saucepan. Bring to a boil over medium-high heat. Remove from heat and pour over the slaw mixture while still hot. Combine the slaw and the dressing well and refrigerate for several hours. Season with the salt and pepper before serving chilled.

PERFECT PICO DE GALLO

This recipe is best if you make it at the peak of summer when tomatoes are ripe and flavorful. If they come from your own backyard garden, the pico will taste all the better.

MAKES about 3½ cups

2 cups diced fresh tomatoes

1 small onion, finely chopped

1 clove garlic, minced

1 to 2 small jalapeño peppers,
   seeded and minced

¼ to ½ cup chopped fresh cilantro

1 Tbsp fresh lemon or lime juice
   (about ½ lemon or lime)

¼ tsp table salt, or to taste

Toss together the tomatoes, onion, garlic, jalapeños, and cilantro. Sprinkle with the lemon or lime juice and salt, and toss again. Serve with tortilla chips.

PERFECT GUACAMOLE

*This simple guacamole disappears from our table very quickly.
You can make it in any quantity using one part Perfect Pico de Gallo
(page 189) to two parts mashed avocado. For best results,
prepare this right before serving.*

MAKES 3 cups

2 cups peeled, pitted, and mashed
  avocado
1 cup Perfect Pico de Gallo
  (page 189)
Table salt to taste

Mix the avocado and pico de gallo together in a bowl. Add the salt (always taste the guacamole using a tortilla chip so you don't overdo the salt), and serve immediately.

PINEAPPLE SALSA

*For a fresh Mediterranean twist, try this sweet, spicy salsa. It's not
just for chips; this salsa goes great with Smoked Mahi-Mahi (page 134).
Avoid using canned pineapple if possible.*

MAKES about 4 cups

2 cups diced fresh pineapple
2 Roma tomatoes, seeded and diced
1 small red onion, finely chopped
1 small jalapeño pepper, seeded
  and minced
1 clove garlic, minced
1 bunch fresh cilantro, rinsed, patted
  dry, and chopped (about ½ cup,
  chopped)
1 lime
Sea salt to taste

In a bowl, combine the pineapple, tomatoes, onion, jalapeño, garlic, and cilantro. Cut the lime in half and squeeze juice over the salsa. Toss to combine and season with salt.

Some of you may be wondering what desserts have to do with smoke cooking outdoors, and I have to say that you are mostly right to wonder. Few desserts work in the smoker, but I have found some that do and I just wanted to share them. This chapter also has a couple of recipes that have nothing to do with smoking, but they are so good I couldn't help throwing them in.

7

DESSERTS

SMOKED APPLE PIE

This is one of those recipes that you will either love a lot or not like at all. A smoked pie looks a lot like a pie that's been baked in the oven; however, when you taste it you will discover a hint of smokiness, as if it had been cooked over an open fire or in a brick wood-fired oven. The pie is especially good if you top it while still warm with some vanilla ice cream.

RECOMMENDED WOOD Apple or alder
ESTIMATED COOK TIME 1½ to 3 hours
SERVES 4

---

4 frozen 9-inch piecrusts, thawed to
    room temperature
4 unpeeled apples, cored and diced
4 tsp fresh lemon juice (about
    ½ lemon)
1 cup (2 sticks) butter, melted
1⅓ cups lightly packed light brown
    sugar
1 tsp ground cinnamon
¼ cup 2% milk

PREPARATION Remove 1 thawed piecrust from its pan and knead it into a ball; divide the ball of dough in half. Form each half into a ball, then roll both out ¼ inch thick on a floured surface. Line the bottom and sides of a 4-inch ramekin or ovenproof dish with one of the halves. Using a pastry or pizza cutter, cut the remaining half into ½-inch strips and set aside. Repeat for all piecrusts.

In a small bowl, toss the apples with the lemon juice. In another bowl, combine the melted butter, brown sugar, and cinnamon; add to the apples and toss to coat. Pour one-quarter of the apple mixture into each piecrust in the ramekins. Lay the reserved dough strips across the top of each pie in a lattice pattern.

When you're finished, press the edges of the strips and the piecrust together around the edge of each ramekin. Use a knife to trim off the excess crust around the outer edges, and brush the top of each crust lightly with some of the milk to help with the browning process.

SMOKING Prepare your smoker for cooking at 275°F. If you are using a gas, an electric, or a charcoal smoker, make sure to have enough wood chips or chunks on hand to produce smoke for about 30 minutes.

Once the smoker is ready, place the ramekins directly on the grate and smoke cook until the apples are soft. The apples can be checked with a toothpick after about one and a half hours, but it may take as long as three hours to get the texture you desire. Serve the pies warm with scoops of vanilla ice cream.

SMOKED APPLE PIE
WITH CABOT CHEDDAR CHEESE

*Apple pie finished with Cabot cheddar cheese on top is a
little different, but I think you will find it so tasty you will
want to try it again. It can also be baked in the oven in the
same manner for a quick and easy everyday dessert.*

RECOMMENDED WOOD Apple

ESTIMATED COOK TIME 1½ to 3 hours

SERVES 4

4 apple pies (see page 194)
Four ¼-inch-thick slices sharp
  Cabot cheddar cheese (or other
  sharp cheddar)

PREPARATION Assemble the apple pies in the ramekins
according to the instructions on page 194.

SMOKING Prepare your smoker for cooking at 275°F. If you
are using a gas, an electric, or a charcoal smoker, make sure to
have enough wood chips or chunks on hand to produce smoke
for about 30 minutes.

Once the smoker is ready, place the ramekins directly on
the grate and smoke cook until the apples are soft. The apples
can be checked with a toothpick after about one and a half
hours, but it may take as long as three hours to get the texture
you desire.

About 15 minutes before the pies are finished cooking,
evenly distribute cheese slices on top of each pie. Keep the pies
warm until ready to serve.

SMOKED BANANAS

I experimented with these for a while until I got them how I like them. With a hint of smoke and the caramelized flavors of brown sugar and honey, this is a dessert you won't soon forget. Use these in a banana split if you are so inclined.

RECOMMENDED WOOD Apple
ESTIMATED COOK TIME 1 hour
SERVES 4

2 ripe bananas
¼ cup honey
½ cup lightly packed light brown sugar
¼ cup (½ stick) butter

PREPARATION Slice the bananas in half lengthwise, making sure to leave the peel attached to each piece so you are left with four long banana boats.

SMOKING Prepare your smoker for cooking at 200°F. If you are using a gas, an electric, or a charcoal smoker, make sure to add enough wood chips or chunks to produce smoke for about 15 to 20 minutes.

Place the bananas directly on the grate, skin side down, and smoke for one hour. Immediately remove from the smoker grate, discard the peels, and place the bananas on a greased cookie sheet. Preheat the broiler to high heat.

FINISHING Brush enough of the honey to coat the entire top of each banana half, then top each half with about 2 Tbsp of the brown sugar. Dot with the butter, then broil the bananas for about four minutes to allow the honey, brown sugar, and butter to caramelize.

Serve immediately topped with vanilla ice cream (you can make your own if you're feeling industrious). For added flavor and texture, sprinkle on some chopped almonds or pecans.

DON'S APPLE-SMOKED PEACHES WITH VANILLA ICE CREAM

My good buddy Don Meadows sent me this recipe and, true to his word, it is delicious to the last bite. Peaches, honey, and ice cream: what more could you ask for? The wood plank used in this recipe does not have to be soaked since it is placed in the smoker and not over a hot grill fire.

RECOMMENDED WOOD Apple or cedar (plank); apple or peach (smoking wood)

ESTIMATED COOK TIME 30 minutes

SERVES 6

---

1 cup honey

⅓ cup lightly packed light brown sugar

6 fresh peaches, pitted and cut in half

PREPARATION Mix together the honey and brown sugar and set aside. Place the peach halves on a smoking plank and drizzle the honey/brown sugar mixture liberally over the peaches.

SMOKING Prepare your smoker for cooking at 250°F. If you are using a charcoal, an electric, or a gas smoker, be sure to have enough wood chips or chunks on hand to produce smoke for about 30 minutes.

Once the smoker is ready, set the wood plank on the grate and smoke cook the peaches for 30 minutes. Serve warm with vanilla ice cream.

JEFF'S GANACHE-INJECTED CHOCOLATE CAKE

Using a meat injector in a dessert recipe is probably not a profoundly new idea, but it produces a cake that is profoundly moist and delicious— almost sinfully so. Ganache is so good and so easy to prepare that once you learn how to make it I am certain you will never use cake icing again. I usually do not make my own cake from scratch; I have found that the quality of boxed cake mixes these days is very good, and they make my life easier when the mood for something sweet strikes. With a little creativity, this can also be done with cupcakes if you prefer.

ESTIMATED COOK TIME 30 minutes

SERVES 12

1 chocolate cake mix
12 oz pkg white chocolate morsels
3 cups heavy cream (35% milk fat)
12 oz pkg semisweet chocolate
  morsels

Bake the cake in the oven according to the package directions. Make sure you don't overcook the cake. I usually remove mine from the oven about five minutes before it's finished baking, since it continues to cook a little after it has been removed from the heat.

While the cake is baking, place the white chocolate morsels into a small mixing bowl. Heat 1½ cups of the heavy cream in a 2-quart saucepan over high heat, and let it come to a boil, whisking occasionally. Once the cream is boiling and the foam rises to the top of the pan, remove it from the heat and pour it over the white chocolate morsels. Wait about 30 seconds, then blend the cream and white chocolate using an electric mixer on medium speed, just until the mixture is smooth and silky. This is the white chocolate ganache.

Repeat this process with the remaining cream and the semisweet chocolate morsels, and set aside. This is the dark chocolate ganache.

After removing the cake from the oven, use a sterilized 1 oz (or larger) meat injector (see page 37) to inject the white chocolate ganache into the cake at 1-inch intervals. To do this, hold the injector at a 45-degree angle, insert it deep into the cake, and gently squeeze the injector until the ganache starts to ooze out of the hole you have made. I usually start at one corner and move across in rows 1 inch apart. Use all of the ganache if possible. Don't worry if it gets messy; the holes will be covered by the dark chocolate ganache in the next step.

(CONTINUED ON PAGE 202)

JEFF'S GANACHE-INJECTED CHOCOLATE CAKE (CONTINUED)

Once you've injected all of the white chocolate ganache, pour the dark chocolate ganache over the top of the cake (or cupcakes) and let it cool on the counter. Once cooled, cover the cake and let it sit for another four to six hours before eating. This allows time for the ganache to thicken a little and for the white chocolate to moisten the inside of the cake completely. Store leftover portions of the cake in a covered cake dish on the counter.

CHOCOLATE NO-BAKE COOKIES

These cookies have become such a staple in our house that I felt compelled to add them to this book. They are a deliciously sweet and satisfying treat after any meal, for a snack, or while waiting on the smoker. It is not uncommon for me to have a stack of these with a large mug of milk during one of my all-night brisket smokes. Follow the recipe carefully and be sure to lick the pot when you're done!

ESTIMATED COOK TIME 10 minutes

MAKES about 24 cookies

---

3 cups quick-cooking oats (regular oats won't work)

½ cup creamy peanut butter

½ cup (1 stick) butter

2½ cups sugar

3 Tbsp cocoa powder

½ cup whole milk (or 2% milk)

1 tsp vanilla extract

Measure out the oats and peanut butter, and set aside. Lay a couple of long strips of waxed paper on the counter or on a table.

Place the butter in a heavy-bottomed saucepan. Add the sugar, cocoa, and milk. Melt over medium-low heat, stirring occasionally with a wooden spoon or rubber spatula. Once melted, bring the mixture to a full boil, and allow to boil for two minutes, stirring often. Use your kitchen timer and be sure to boil for the full two minutes.

Remove from the heat and quickly stir in the peanut butter and vanilla, whisking until blended. Fold in the oatmeal until evenly coated with chocolate, and drop by large spoonfuls onto the waxed paper. (If you want to measure, try using a ¼-cup scoop for medium-large cookies.) Allow to cool completely before serving.

To smoke cheese, you need to create smoke while keeping the temperature of the smoker low enough so the cheese does not melt. This can be a bit of a challenge if you don't have the right equipment, but I have outlined several methods of cold smoking on pages 46–47 that should help.

The recipes that follow provide smoking instructions for three different cheese products, but the methods can work with many other varieties of cheeses.

8

CHEESE

SMOKED CHEDDAR CHEESE

*Of all the smoked cheeses, cheddar is definitely my all-time favorite.
Once you taste the home-smoked version, you just won't be content to
buy the pre-smoked stuff any longer. Gouda, Muenster, Edam, mozzarella,
Swiss, and pepper Jack are also great choices for this recipe.*

RECOMMENDED WOOD Apple, alder,
  or cherry
ESTIMATED COOK TIME 4 hours
SMOKES Two 8 oz blocks of cheese

Two 8 oz blocks cheddar cheese

Using one of the cold-smoking methods described on pages
46–47, set up your smoker to maintain a temperature of less
than 90°F.

Place the blocks of cheese directly on the grate and apply
light smoke for about four hours. Remove the cheese from the
grate and place it into a Ziploc bag. Store the smoked cheese
in the refrigerator for two weeks before eating it to allow the
smoke flavor to disperse throughout the cheese.

SMOKED CREAM CHEESE

*Who would have thought of smoking something like cream cheese?
For a new twist on dessert or even for a spread or dip, the hint
of smoke in this cheese will be something you are sure to enjoy.*

RECOMMENDED WOOD Apple, alder,
or cherry

ESTIMATED COOK TIME 2 hours

SMOKES Two 8 oz blocks of cream
cheese

Two 8 oz pkgs cream cheese

Set up the smoker for cold smoking using one of the methods outlined on pages 46–47. Place the cream cheese in a pie plate or on another flat surface, and set it on the smoker grate. Apply light smoke for about two hours, making sure to keep the heat at no more than 75°F to 80°F, since cream cheese melts very easily.

After removing the cheese from the grate, mix it with a spoon or spatula to help distribute the smoke flavor, then reform it into two blocks. For the best-tasting result, place the cream cheese into a Ziploc bag and store it in the refrigerator for four to ten days before eating it or using it in a recipe.

SMOKED CHEESE STICKS

Cheese sticks come in cheddar, pepper Jack, mozzarella, or various cheese blends. Smoke them just like any other cheese, then wrap them individually in plastic wrap or place them in Ziploc bags as handy snacks for kids and adults alike.

RECOMMENDED WOOD Apple, alder, cherry, or oak

ESTIMATED COOK TIME 1 hour

SMOKES 24 cheese sticks

---

24 cheese sticks (not string cheese)

Prepare the smoker for cold smoking using one of the methods on pages 46–47. Lay the cheese sticks on the grate with about a ½ inch between them to allow the smoke to get to all parts of the cheese. Apply light smoke for one hour, making sure to maintain a smoker temperature of less than 90°F.

Remove the cheese sticks from the grate and place them in a Ziploc bag in the refrigerator for four to ten days to let the smoke flavor disperse throughout the cheese.

WHERE TO PURCHASE SMOKING EQUIPMENT & SUPPLIES

A-Maze-N-Smoker	www.amazenproducts.com
Backwoods	www.backwoods-smoker.com
BBQ Guru	www.bbqguru.com
Bell Fabrications	www.bellfab.com
Big Green Egg	www.biggreenegg.com
Big John Grills & Rotisseries	www.bigjohngrills.com
Bradley	www.bradleysmoker.com
Brinkmann	www.brinkmann.net
Cajun Injector	www.cajuninjector.com
Char-Broil/New Braunfels	www.charbroil.com
Cookers and Grills	www.cookersandgrills.com
Cookshack	www.cookshack.com
Gator Pit	www.gatorpit.net
Horizon	www.hightide.com/horizon2
Klose	www.bbqpits.com
Landmann	www.landmann-usa.com
Lang	www.pigroast.com
Masterbuilt	www.masterbuilt.com
Ole Hickory Pits	www.olehickorypits.com
Pitt's & Spitt's	www.pittsandspitts.net
Rock's Bar-b-que	www.rocksbarbque.com
Smoke Daddy	www.smokedaddyinc.com
Smoke Hollow	www.olp-inc.com
Southern Pride	www.southernpride.com
Stump's Smokers	www.stumpssmokers.com
Tejas Smokers	www.tejassmokers.com
Traeger	www.traegergrills.com
Weber	www.weber.com

I am a big fan of Amazon.com. I probably spend way too much time and money there, but just about anything I need, whether it be a book or a crazy item like a jalapeño pepper roaster, can be found with relative ease and, in most cases, with free shipping. A few brick and mortar retailers also sell smoking equipment and accessories online. My favorite online sources are:

- Amazon.com
- BassPro.com
- HomeDepot.com
- Lowes.com
- Target.com
- Walmart.com

METRIC CONVERSION CHARTS

TEMPERATURE

Imperial	Metric
33°F	0.6°C
35°F	1.7°C
39°F	3.9°C
40°F	4.4°C
50°F	10°C
90°F	32°C
125°F	52°C
140°F	60°C
145°F	63°C
150°F	66°C
160°F	71°C

Imperial	Metric
165°F	74°C
180°F	82°C
185°F	85°C
190°F	88°C
195°F	91°C
200°F	93°C
205°F	96°C
210°F	99°C
212°F	100°C
225°F	107°C
240°F	116°C

Imperial	Metric
250°F	121°C
275°F	135°C (140°C for ovens)
300°F	149°C
325°F	163°C
350°F	177°C (180°C for ovens)
375°F	191°C
400°F	204°C
900°F	482°C

VOLUME

Imperial	Metric
⅛ tsp	0.5 mL
¼ tsp	1 mL
½ tsp	2 mL
1 tsp	5 mL
½ Tbsp	7.5 mL
2 tsp	10 mL
1 Tbsp	15 mL
4 tsp	20 mL
2 Tbsp	30 mL
3 Tbsp	45 mL
¼ cup	60 mL

Imperial	Metric
5 Tbsp	75 mL
⅓ cup	80 mL
½ cup	125 mL
⅔ cup	160 mL
¾ cup	185 mL
1 cup	250 mL
1¼ cups	310 mL
1½ cups	375 mL
1¾ cups	435 mL
2 cups	500 mL
4 cups	1 L

Imperial	Metric
6 cups	1.5 L
8 cups	2 L
1 quart	1.1 L
2 quarts (½ gallon)	2.3 L
1 gallon	4.5 L
1½ gallons	6.8 L
2 gallons	9 L
2½ gallons	11.4 L
3 gallons	13.6 L
5 gallons	22.7 L

WEIGHT

Imperial	Metric	Imperial	Metric	Imperial	Metric
1 oz	28 g	1 lb (16 oz)	454 g	5 lb	2.2 kg
1½ oz	43 g	20 oz	567 g	6 lb	2.7 kg
2 oz	57 g	2 lb	900 g	7 lb	3.2 kg
4 oz (¼ lb)	114 g	2½ lb	1.1 kg	9 lb	4 kg
8 oz (½ lb)	227 g	3 lb	1.4 kg	12 lb	5.4 kg
12 oz	340 g	4 lb	1.8 kg		

LENGTH

Imperial	Metric	Imperial	Metric	Imperial	Metric
¼ inch	6 mm	6 inches	15 cm	14 inches	35 cm
½ inch	1 cm	7 inches	18 cm	15 inches	38 cm
¾ inch	2 cm	8 inches	20 cm	16 inches	40 cm
1 inch	2.5 cm	9 inches	23 cm	18 inches	46 cm
1½ inches	4 cm	10 inches	25 cm	20 inches	50 cm
2 inches	5 cm	11 inches	28 cm	22 inches	55 cm
3 inches	8 cm	1 foot (12 inches)	30 cm	22½ inches	57 cm
4 inches	10 cm	13 inches	33 cm	6 feet	1.8 m
5 inches	12 cm			10 feet	3 m

CAN SIZES

Imperial	Metric	Imperial	Metric
4 oz can	114 mL can	15 oz can	426 mL can
8 oz can	237 mL can	24 oz bottle	682 mL bottle
10½ oz can	298 mL can	28 oz can	796 mL can
12 oz can	355 mL can	55 oz can	1.56 L can